*access*

# WAR *and* PEACE: INTERNATIONAL RELATIONS 1919–39

*Second Edition*

*David G. Williamson*

Stoughton

ODDER HEADLINE GROUP

## Acknowledgements

The publishers would like to thank the following individuals, institutions and companies for permission to reproduce copyright illustrations in this book:

Punch Ltd: pages 20, 34, 72; Bettman/CORBIS: page 57; Hulton-Deutsch/CORBIS: page 71; Sir David Low, *Evening Standard* and Atlantic Syndication, Cartoon Study Centre, University of Kent, Canterbury, CT2 7NU: page 110; Hulton Archive: page 131; Hulton Archive/Getty Images: page 133; Clifford Berryman, *Washington Star*/Library of Congress. Nazi-Soviet Pact October, 1939: page 137.

The publishers would also like to thank the following for permission to reproduce material in this book:

The Economist Newspaper Limited, London, for an extract from *The Millennium Issue*, by M Macmillan (1999) used on page 147; Princeton University Press for extracts from *Recasting Bourgeois Europe* by C S Maier (1988) used on page 89.

Every effort has been made to trace and acknowledge ownership of copyright. The publishers will be glad to make suitable arrangements with any copyright holders whom it has not been possible to contact.

Orders: please contact Bookpoint Ltd, 130 Milton Park, Abingdon, Oxon OX14 4SB. Telephone: (44) 01235 827720. Fax: (44) 01235 400454. Lines are open from 9.00–6.00, Monday to Saturday, with a 24 hour message answering service. You can also order through our website www.hodderheadline.co.uk.

*British Library Cataloguing in Publication Data*
A catalogue record for this title is available from the British Library

ISBN 0 340 857 92 7

First published 1994
Second edition published 2003
Impression number   10 9 8 7 6 5 4 3 2 1
Year                2009 2008 2007 2006 2005 2004 2003

The cover illustration is *The Trail of War*, 1919 (depicting destroyed Turkish aircraft) by Sydney Carline (1888–1929), courtesy of York City Art Gallery/Bridgeman Art gallery, London.

Produced by Gray Publishing, Tunbridge Wells
Printed in Great Britain for Hodder & Stoughton Educational, a division of Hodder Headline Plc, 338 Euston Road, London NW1 3BH by Bath Press Ltd.

# Contents

# Preface

## To the general reader

Although the *Access to History* series has been designed with the needs of students studying the subject at higher examination levels very much in mind, it also has a great deal to offer the general reader. The main body of the text (i.e. ignoring the 'Study Guides' at the ends of chapters) forms a readable and yet stimulating survey of a coherent topic as studied by historians. However, each author's aim has not merely been to provide a clear explanation of what happened in the past (for interest and to inform): it has also been assumed that most readers wish to be stimulated into thinking further about the topic and to form opinions of their own about the significance of the events that are described and discussed (to be challenged). Thus, although no prior knowledge of the topic is expected on the reader's part, she or he is treated as an intelligent and thinking person throughout. The author tends to share ideas and possibilities with the reader, rather than passing on numbers of so-called 'historical truths'.

## To the student reader

Although advantage has been taken of the publication of a second edition to ensure the results of recent research are reflected in the text, the main alteration from the first edition is the inclusion of new features, and the modification of existing ones, aimed at assisting you in your study of the topic at AS level, A level and Higher. Two features are designed to assist you during your first reading of a chapter. The *Points to Consider* section following each chapter title is intended to focus your attention on the main theme(s) of the chapter, and the issues box following most section headings alerts you to the question or questions to be dealt with in the section. The *Working on ...* section at the end of each chapter suggests ways of gaining maximum benefit from the chapter.

There are many ways in which the series can be used by students studying history at a higher level. It will, therefore, be worthwhile thinking about your own study strategy before you start your work on this book. Obviously, your strategy will vary depending on the aim you have in mind, and the time for study that is available to you.

If, for example, you want to acquire a general overview of the topic in the shortest possible time, the following approach will probably be the most effective:

**1** Read Chapter 1. As you do so, keep in mind the issues raised in the *Points to Consider* section.

**2** Read the *Points to Consider* section at the beginning of Chapter 2 and decide whether it is necessary for you to read this chapter.

**3** If it is, read the chapter, stopping at each heading or sub-heading to note down the main points that have been made. Often, the best way of doing this is to answer the question(s) posed in the Key Issues boxes.

**4** Repeat Stage 2 (and Stage 3 where appropriate) for all the other chapters.

If, however, your aim is to gain a thorough grasp of the topic, taking however much time is necessary to do so, you may benefit from carrying out the same procedure with each chapter, as follows:

**1** Try to read the chapter in one sitting. As you do this, bear in mind any advice given in the *Points to Consider* section.

**2** Study the flow diagram at the end of the chapter, ensuring that you understand the general 'shape' of what you have just read.

**3** Read the *Working on ...* section and decide what further work you need to do on the chapter. In particularly important sections of the book, this is likely to involve reading the chapter a second time and stopping at each heading and sub-heading to think about (and probably to write a summary of) what you have just read.

**4** Attempt the *Source-based questions* section. It will sometimes be sufficient to think through your answers, but additional understanding will often be gained by forcing yourself to write them down.

When you have finished the main chapters of the book, study the 'Further Reading' section and decide what additional reading (if any) you will do on the topic.

This book has been designed to help make your studies both enjoyable and successful. If you can think of ways in which this could have been done more effectively, please contact us. In the meantime, we hope that you will gain greatly from your study of history.

*Keith Randell & Robert Pearce*

# 1 International Relations 1919–39: An Introduction

## POINTS TO CONSIDER

The point of this introductory chapter is to help you understand the overall pattern of events before studying international relations in the period 1919–39 in greater detail. First of all it outlines the way the peace treaties reshaped Europe and the Middle East and how the victorious powers attempted to create a peace-keeping organisation in the form of the League of Nations. It stresses the significance of the USA's refusal both to ratify the Treaty and to join the League of Nations. It then looks at how Britain and France attempted to enforce the peace treaties in the immediate postwar period and how the Ruhr and Chanak crises compelled them to make some limited concessions to Germany and Turkey. This helped lay the basis for a brief period of peaceful cooperation between the great European powers and enabled the League to function with some degree of effectiveness during the years 1925–9. The second half of the chapter briefly explains the disastrous impact of the Great Depression on international politics and how it brought Hitler to power and encouraged expansionist policies in Italy and Japan, which destroyed the postwar system and ultimately led to the outbreak of the Second World War.

## KEY DATES

| | |
|---|---|
| **1919** | Treaty of Versailles |
| **1920** | Treaty of Sèvres |
| **1923** | Ruhr Crisis |
| **1925** | Locarno Treaties |
| **1929** | Hague Conference |
| **1931** | Japanese attack on Manchuria |
| **1933** | Hitler appointed Chancellor of Germany |
| **1935** | Abyssinia invaded by Italy |
| **1936** | Rhineland remilitarised by Germany |
| **1938** | German annexation of Austria |
| | The Sudeten Crisis |
| **1939** | German occupation of Bohemia and Moravia |
| | Nazi–Soviet Pact |
| | Britain and France declare war on Germany. |

# 1 Problems of Interpretation

> **KEY ISSUES** How should the interwar period be assessed by
> historians? Was it just an armistice between the two 'German wars'?

It is always a temptation for historians to divide past events into neat
eras or epochs. The period 1919–39 seems to fit easily into such a pattern. It starts with the victorious conclusion of major war fought to
prevent German domination of Europe and it ends with the outbreak
of a second and more bloody conflict waged for the same purpose. In
short, the years 1919–39 seem to be a prolonged armistice between
the two great German wars. Winston Churchill and many of his
contemporaries, thinking of the great struggle in central Europe that
raged between 1618 and 1648, characterised the whole period
between 1914 and 1945 as a new 'Thirty Years War'. At first glance this
description seems appropriate. After all, Germany was not destroyed
in 1918 and the peace settlements of 1919–20 appeared to many
people to be just a temporary truce before a new war broke out.
Marshal Foch, the Commander-in-Chief of the Allied armies in 1918,
described the Treaty of Versailles as an armistice that would only last
for 20 years. Between 1919 and 1923 France went to the very edge of
war in an attempt to enforce the peace settlement on Germany, and
10 years later, with Hitler's seizure of power, the countdown to the
Second World War seemed to have begun.

However, is it accurate to describe this whole period as nothing but
a prolonged armistice? Does this not, in P.M.H. Bell's words, 'squeeze
out of our history the men and events between the wars, as though
they were nothing more than ghostly inhabitants of an extended half-
time interval'?[1] There were many similarities between German war
aims in both wars, but this does not necessarily mean that the two wars
were really the same conflict, although some historians like Fritz
Fischer would imply that they were. It is possible to argue that
between 1924 and 1930 American and European statesmen did
manage to make the Versailles settlement work and were well on the
way to solving the German problem peacefully, and that consequently
the Second World War was far from inevitable. Perhaps it was the
economic depression of 1929–33, and not the unfinished business of
1918, which, by bringing Hitler to power, caused the Second World
War. On the other hand the disruption of the world economy by the
First World War was a major reason why the Depression wreaked such
havoc on the global economies. Some historians stress that it is a sim-
plification of complex events to assume that a world war was
inevitable once Hitler came to power. Hitler certainly had long-term
plans for the destruction of the Soviet Union (USSR) and the large
scale annexation of Russian territory, but did he also want to fight
Britain and France? In 1939 it can also be argued that these two

powers went to war against Germany to maintain what was left of the Versailles system and their position as great powers.

So far we have only discussed the consequences of the end of the first 'German war' and the causes of the next, but there were other conflicts in eastern Europe and Russia (1918–21), Abyssinia and Spain (1935–9), and the Far East (from 1937 onwards) that all helped collectively to destabilise the peace settlements and weaken Europe. However much historians may debate the causes of the two world wars, all agree on the irreparable damage they did to Europe's prosperity and position in the world.

# 2 The Peace Settlements

> **KEY ISSUES** In what ways did the Peace Treaties reflect the intentions of the victorious powers? How effective were the peace treaties in laying the foundations for a new peaceful postwar world?

The peace treaties were negotiated under very difficult circumstances. Civil war had broken out in Russia in the aftermath of the Bolshevik revolution, while the collapse of Germany and its allies exposed central Europe to the threat of Communism. The end of hostilities confronted the victorious powers with the most complex problems that needed urgent solutions. Yet apart from a general assumption that independent national states in eastern Europe and the Balkans would replace the old Austro-Hungarian empire, there was no unanimous agreement amongst the Allies what these solutions should be:

- President Wilson of the USA placed enormous emphasis on the League of Nations and believed that it would prove to be the key to creating a peaceful postwar world. He also believed in national self-determination, and the creation where possible of independent nation states;
- the French prime minister, Clemenceau, was anxious to weaken Germany in every possible way;
- Britain, on the other hand, as a result of the surrender and subsequent destruction of the German fleet and the collapse of Germany's global trade, had already seen its main war aims fulfilled, and now wanted a peaceful united Germany, which would both act as a barrier to the spread of Bolshevism from the east and as a market for British goods;
- Italy and Japan aimed to maximise their war time gains. Italy above all wanted to force the *Entente* to honour the Treaty of London of 1915, which had promised it large gains in Istria and Dalmatia.

The Treaty of Versailles was essentially a compromise between British and French policies on how to treat Germany. It was criticised almost immediately in Britain and America for being too harsh, while to the French it did not go far enough. Later in the 1930s it was commonly regarded as the seedbed for the reemergence of German nationalism under Hitler, but it can equally be argued that it was not tough enough. It left a potentially strong Germany still intact in the middle of Europe surrounded by a series of small weak new states. It was less harsh than the treaty that the Germans signed with the defeated Russians at Brest Litovsk in March 1918, and it still left a united Germany capable of revival as a great European power.

Once the Treaty of Versailles was signed, Allied officials remained in Paris to wrestle with the difficult problems created by the collapse of the Austro-Hungarian and Turkish Empires in the Balkans and the Middle East. In the four treaties signed with the successor states they tried to create a new structure of nation states:

- the Treaty of St Germain reduced Austria to a small rump state of 8 million people and allocated its former non-German-speaking territories to the new states of Czechoslovakia and what was later to be called Yugloslavia;
- by the Treaty of Trianon, Hungary lost over two-thirds of its territory to Czechslovakia, Romania and Yugoslavia;
- through the Treaty of Neuilly, Bulgaria had to cede considerable territories to Greece and Serbia;
- of all the peace treaties the most harsh was the Treaty of Sèvres with Turkey: this handed over its Middle eastern territories to Britain and France as League of Nations mandates (see Glossary, page 155), and sought to confine the new state to its ethnic core;
- The constitution of the League of Nations, which President Wilson optimistically hoped would solve all the inevitable problems of detail that the treaties had left unsolved, was included in the first section of all five treaties.

The Allied statesmen in Paris were neither able to fix Poland's eastern frontiers nor to secure the independence of the Baltic states as long as the Russian civil war and the Russo-Polish conflict lasted. The USSR only recognised the independence of the Baltic states in 1920 and the Soviet–Polish borders could only be finalised once the Polish and Soviet governments negotiated peace by the Treaty of Riga in March 1921.

## 3 Postwar Problems 1920–3

> **KEY ISSUES** What were the problems that confronted the peace-makers in the immediate postwar years? How effectively were the treaties enforced?

As we have seen, the Treaty of Versailles was a compromise between Britain and France, which left Germany essentially intact. This might have worked had the American Senate not refused to accept the principle of American involvement in the League. Its failure to ratify the Treaty of Versailles ensured that all plans for an Anglo-American guarantee of France were abandoned. Thus it was now left to Britain and France to enforce the peace, but both had fundamentally different approaches. Almost as soon as the Treaty was signed, these two powers began unofficially to revise it. The French tried to exploit every loophole in the treaty to compensate for what they saw as its leniency, while the British followed a different approach and attempted to appease the Germans by generously interpreting key clauses of the treaty. There were thus bitter arguments over:

- reparation payments;
- disarmament;
- the implementation of the Treaty in Eastern Europe, particularly in Upper Silesia.

Anglo-French disagreements over Germany came to a head in January 1923 when the French, on the pretext of late German reparation deliveries in coal and timber, occupied the Ruhr. Their intention was not only to force Germany to honour its reparation obligations but also to split off the Rhineland from Germany by creating a French satellite state there. Britain adopted a policy of 'benevolent passivity' and refused to cooperate with the French, but it was only in early 1924, when it became clear that French policy was failing, that Britain together with the USA was able to bring the Ruhr conflict to an end by persuading both France and Germany to accept the Dawes Plan.

In attempting to carry out the Treaty of Sèvres with Turkey the Allies had even greater problems. As with Versailles, Sèvres was an Anglo-French compromise, but this time it was the French who wished to be more lenient towards Turkey, if only because they had lent its government huge sums before the war, while the British were more interested in partitioning the Ottoman empire and building up the power of Greece at Turkey's expense. Sèvres was a harsh treaty that the Turks might just have accepted had it been imposed quickly, but by August 1920, when it was signed, the Sultan's government was faced by a nationalist rebellion led by the formidable Mustapha Kemal. Over the next 2 years Kemal was able to recapture Turkish Armenia, smash the Greek occupying army in Smyrna, and then force the Allies to abandon the treaty of Sèvres and negotiate a new agreement at Lausanne in 1923.

The immediate postwar years also showed that the peace treaties with Bulgaria and the successor states to the Austro-Hungary Empire created as many problems as they solved, since they came nowhere near to forming the compact nation states, which President Wilson had wished to create. Instead, there were numerous racial minorities trapped within each state and the territorial settlement had also created intense rivalries between the new states, which led to frequent outbreaks of violence and serious diplomatic incidents.

# 4 A Peaceful Interlude, 1924–30

> **KEY ISSUES** How much progress did the European powers make towards solving the bitter postwar legacy in Europe? To what extent did the USA abandon its policy of isolation?

Neither Germany nor France emerged the winner from the Ruhr conflict. Without British assistance it was clear that France could not impose its will on Germany, while the German government had done irreparable damage to its finances by attempting to oppose the French occupation with a passive resistance campaign by the Ruhr workers. This was financed by printing money, which finally triggered ruinous hyper-inflation. Both sides were therefore ready to accept the Anglo-American Dawes Plan, which, by arranging for an international loan to be granted to Germany and recommending an initially more gradual scale of repayment for reparations, gave Germany the chance to recover economically.

The acceptance of the Dawes Plan created one of the basic preconditions for European recovery. The other precondition was the signature of the Locarno Treaty in October 1925 by France, Germany, Britain and Italy. Gustav Stresemann, the German Foreign Minister, had come to the conclusion that Germany could only regain its position as a European great power by reassuring the French that it accepted the postwar settlement in the west, while reserving the right to seek peaceful adjustments in the east. The Locarno Treaty thus committed these four European powers to guarantee the continued demilitarisation of the Rhineland and the post-1919 frontiers between Belgium and Germany and between France and Germany.

The Treaty did not immediately remove mutual Franco-German suspicions, but it had made a start, and, except for hardline nationalists in both France and Germany, the new 'Locarno spirit' was celebrated enthusiastically throughout western Europe. Over the next 5 years it looked at last as if the foundations for a more lasting European peace were being laid:

- In January 1926 the British and French evacuated the Cologne Zone;
- 10 months later Germany joined the Council of the League of Nations;
- in 1927 the Allied Disarmament Commission was withdrawn from Germany;
- at the Hague Conference in 1929 the Young Plan, which cut the overall total sum of reparations that Germany had to pay, was accepted by Berlin, and the British and French agreed to pull out completely from the Rhineland 5 years earlier than they were committed to do by the Treaty of Versailles;
- a plan, which was admittedly only vague and non-committal, was also drawn up by the French Foreign Minister, Aristide Briand, for

a European Customs union and a common currency, which in principle was supported by Gustav Stresemann.

During these years there were also signs that the USA might begin again to play a role in world affairs. Washington not only helped to formulate the Dawes Plan but also joined the League of Nation's Preparatory Commission, which was set up to prepare for the World Disarmament conference. In 1928 the American Secretary of State, Frank Kellogg, together with Briand, also drafted an international anti-war treaty, the so-called Kellogg–Briand Peace Pact, which 50 nations had joined by 1933. Although the USSR was essentially hostile to what it regarded as the imperialist and capitalist west, it lacked the strength to be a real threat and also needed to trade with the world's industrial nations.

# 5  The League of Nations

> **KEY ISSUE**  How did the League work and how successful was it?

The first section of all the peace treaties contained the Covenant of the League of Nations and committed both the Allies and the defeated powers to setting up the League of Nations. Its 26 articles briefly outlined its constitution and how it would work. It would consist of:

- the Assembly in which both the great and small powers would only have one vote each;
- the Council, which initially had four permanent members: Britain, France, Italy and Japan;
- a permanent Secretariat;
- a permanent international court.

It was given ultimate responsibility for the ex-enemy colonies, which the *Entente* powers administered on its behalf. Part of its remit was also to set up international offices dealing with labour, health, transport, etc. The primary aim of the League, however, was to prevent war. Its constitution contained provision for solving disputes between states and even for appealing to members to use force to 'protect the Covenants of the League' (Article 16). The problem, however, was that the League was dependent on the willingness of its members to cooperate and outlaw war. If they refused to cooperate, there was, in the final analysis, nothing it could do. It was initially handicapped by the absence of Germany, the USA and the USSR from its membership. Germany joined in 1926 and the USSR in 1933, but the refusal of the world's most wealthy state, the USA, to become a member seriously weakened its effectiveness. The League was at its most effective during the period 1925–30 when Britain, Germany and France all cooperated closely on the Council. It was then that progress was made in preparing for a world disarmament conference, but the Great Depression rapidly brought this brief 'golden age' to an end.

## 6 The Consequences of the Great Depression

> **KEY ISSUE** What was the impact of the Great Depression on international politics?

The Great Depression was a watershed in interwar history. It plunged the whole world into an economic crisis at a time when economic recovery was still fragile. America, which had been drawing closer to the League, retreated back into isolation, while in Japan the intensely nationalist officer corps gained increasing influence over the government. The economic crisis in Germany was made worse by the policies of Chancellor Brüning, who was determined to exploit the devastating impact of the Depression to convince the western powers that Germany could no longer afford to pay reparations. This policy had some success, but it also helped bring Hitler to power.

As global trade collapsed, the major trading powers tried to protect their home markets, by setting up tariff barriers that would keep out foreign imports. The British and French with their large colonial empires, as well as the huge states of the USA and USSR enjoyed a major advantage over the Germans, Japanese and Italians, who increasingly began to demand their own spheres of interest or empires, which they would be able to dominate economically:

- the desire to possess the coal mines and supplies of iron ore in Manchuria was one of the main reason why the Japanese seized Manchuria in 1931;
- the desire for 'living space' in eastern Europe, above all in Russia, was the driving force behind Hitler's foreign policy;
- the Depression also prompted Mussolini to draw up plans for the occupation of Abyssinia.

## 7 The Collapse of the League and the Weakening of the Versailles System

> **KEY ISSUES** Why was the League unable to stop the aggressive policies of Japan and Italy, 1931–6? Why were Britain and France unable to stop Hitler from breaking key clauses of the Treaty of Versailles?

When Japan annexed Manchuria in 1931 and Italy invaded Abyssinia in 1935, the League faced the two most decisive challenges to its authority. Its failure to uphold its principles in face of open aggression effectively ended any claims to influence it had on world affairs. These two crises highlighted the potential weaknesses of the League. It was not a world government with its own armies and was completely dependent on the great powers to stop aggression. In 1931, in the middle of the Depression, neither Britain nor France was ready for major military operations in Manchuria, and the most powerful state with bases in the Pacific, the USA, was not even a member of the League. It was not surprising, then, that the League was unable to enforce the recommendations of its Commission of Enquiry, which it had sent to Manchuria.

The Manchurian crisis certainly weakened the League and the whole concept of collective security, but this did not necessarily mean that the Versailles system would collapse in Europe. Initially when Hitler came to power and began openly to rearm, Italy, France and, reluctantly, even Britain began to draw closer together, but this cooperation was shattered by Italy's invasion of Abyssinia. Essentially, the two western democracies pursued a policy that produced the worst of all possible results. Either London and Paris could have decided to sacrifice Abyssinia and thus encouraged Italy to continue to cooperate with them in containing Nazi Germany, or else they could have used their naval superiority in the Mediterranean to intercept Italian forces on the way across to the Gulf of Aden and the Italian bases in Eritrea. In fact by supporting through the League only a policy of very moderate sanctions against Italy, Mussolini was not prevented from completing his conquest of Abyssinia. He was able to evade the impact of the sanctions by looking to the German government for both the supply of raw materials and diplomatic backing. The concentration of Britain and France on the Abyssinian crisis and the new dependence of Mussolini on Berlin gave Hitler a marvellous opportunity to move troops into the demilitarised Rhineland and so deliver a devastating blow to the Versailles system.

Over the following year, 1936–7 the balance of power globally began to swing against western democracies:

- In July 1936 the Spanish Civil war began, and German and Italian forces were sent to assist the Spanish Nationalists under General Franco;
- In October the Rome–Berlin Axis was signed;
- This was followed in November by the German–Japanese Anti-Comintern Pact, which Italy joined a year later in November 1937;
- In July 1937 Japan attacked China and began a Far Eastern War which ended only in August 1945.

## 8 The Outbreak of the Second World War

> **KEY ISSUES** What were the causes of the Second World War? Why did the policy of appeasement fail?

Between early 1938 and September 1939, when war broke out over Poland, the diplomatic situation in Europe rapidly deteriorated. In

March 1938 Hitler exploited an unexpected opportunity to annex Austria (the *Anschluss*); and then, in September at the Munich Conference, only the offer of the German-speaking Sudetenland and the threat of war temporarily persuaded Hitler to back down and not destroy Czechoslovakia. However, in March 1939 he was able to achieve this, when he took advantage of growing ethnic tension between the Czechs and Slovaks to intervene on the latter's behalf. This action galvanised Britain, which was supported by France, to guarantee first Poland, then Greece and Romania, in an effort to build up an anti-Nazi front in Eastern Europe. The Polish government's refusal to agree to the return of the German territory awarded to it in 1919, coupled with the Anglo-French guarantee, convinced Hitler that Poland would have to be destroyed before he could begin to realise his territorial aims in eastern Europe. The key to the coming crisis over Poland was the position of the USSR. If Stalin supported the western powers, Germany faced a war on two fronts, but if Hitler could negotiate some sort of a deal with USSR, the very power that he had up to this point consistently characterised as Germany's main enemy, it seemed very unlikely that Britain and France would risk coming to Poland's rescue. Consequently in the summer of 1939 both the western powers and Germany sought an agreement with Moscow. It was Hitler who was successful as, in exchange for Soviet neutrality in a German–Polish war, he was able to able to offer Stalin the prospect of eastern Poland.

Why then, despite the Nazi–Soviet Pact, did Britain and France declare war on Germany? Was it an 'accident' in that Hitler did not leave himself enough time to drive a wedge between Poland and its allies in Paris and London, or did Hitler in fact want to eliminate Poland as an independent power even if it meant war with the West? France and Britain would certainly have preferred a negotiated settlement, but they did not want the humiliation of a second Munich. If war was inevitable, the British government believed that it was better to fight it sooner rather later before Germany had grown even more powerful.

## 9 Basic Issues of International Relations, 1919–39

> **KEY ISSUE** What are the basic questions to ask about the course of international relations, 1919–39?

In order to understand this complex period, it is important for you to keep the following basic questions in mind as your read through the book:

i  Did the peace settlements of 1919–20 make a second world war inevitable?

ii   Was the whole interwar period just an 'armistice' between the two German wars?
iii  Or did the Locarno era of 1925–9 really begin to lay the foundations for a period of peace and reconciliation?
iv   Why was the Great Depression a turning point in international history?
v    Did Hitler's rise to power make another European war inevitable?
vi   Why were Britain and France unsuccessful in containing Japan in the Far East, and Italy in Abysinnia ?
vii  Why did appeasement fail?
viii Why did Britain and France go to war for the sake of Poland in September 1939?

## Reference

1   P.M.H. Bell, *The Origins of The Second World War in Europe* (Longman, London, 1986), p. 31.

## Summary Diagram
### An Overview of International Relations between the Two Wars

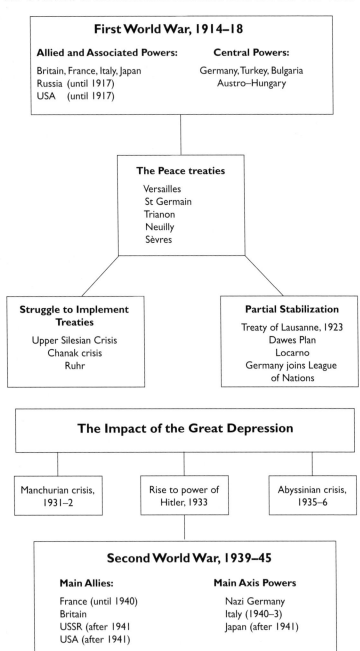

**First World War, 1914–18**

**Allied and Associated Powers:**

Britain, France, Italy, Japan
Russia (until 1917)
USA (until 1917)

**Central Powers:**

Germany, Turkey, Bulgaria
Austro–Hungary

**The Peace treaties**

Versailles
St Germain
Trianon
Neuilly
Sèvres

**Struggle to Implement Treaties**

Upper Silesian Crisis
Chanak crisis
Ruhr

**Partial Stabilization**

Treaty of Lausanne, 1923
Dawes Plan
Locarno
Germany joins League
of Nations

**The Impact of the Great Depression**

Manchurian crisis,
1931–2

Rise to power of
Hitler, 1933

Abyssinian crisis,
1935–6

**Second World War, 1939–45**

**Main Allies:**

France (until 1940)
Britain
USSR (after 1941
USA (after 1941)

**Main Axis Powers**

Nazi Germany
Italy (1940–3)
Japan (after 1941)

## Working on Chapter 1

This chapter provides an overview of the diplomatic situation, 1919–39, both in Europe and globally. Before moving on to the next chapter, write out the time line on page 1, adding to it any significant dates that you have found in this chapter. If possible, compile the chronology on a computer, so that you can add to it as your read on further into the book. Also, as far you can at this stage, write out brief answers to the Key Issue questions in Sections 1–9.

At the end of each chapter in this book there are structured and essay questions with advice on how to answer them. Here is some introductory information on how to cope with these two types of exam questions:

Structured questions usually require two different responses:

i   In some of the AS papers you will be asked to 'outline', which in fact means describe, a sequence of events. To gain full marks in this sort of question you need to know the facts and make sure that you cover the full range of *relevant* events.

ii   Then instead of outlining a sequence of events, you will be set a question which requires more thought, analysis and explanation. You might, for example, be asked to explain why a particular event occurred and/or *what* its consequences were.

In some of the exam papers you will also have to write essays on more wide-ranging topics. A typical question could be: 'Was Germany responsible for causing the Second World War?' When preparing an essay of this sort, it would be a good idea to take the following steps:

- Ask yourself what are the key words. In this case they are: 'Germany … causing … War'.
- Then decide on the key themes of your argument and how you will effectively use them to answer the question. Here, the key themes are: Hitler's aims and intentions, the consequences of the Treaty of Versailles and also the determination of Britain and France not to allow Germany a completely free hand in eastern Europe. Can you think of any more? Remember that you must flesh out these key points with accurate evidence, the relevance of which you must explain. If you just write down the facts without showing why they are relevant, you will lose a lot of marks. Remember, too, that you are required to construct an *argument* backed up with relevant evidence. Before you start writing the essay, it is a good idea to draw up a plan, although in an exam, this will inevitably have to be a very brief list of the key points you wish to stress.
- Your essay should have a short introductory paragraph in which you introduce the *gist* of your main arguments. The paragraph should be relevant, interesting and concise.

- Then in the main section of your essay, you should develop these arguments further, backed up with well-chosen evidence. To ensure that you do not waffle, begin each paragraph with a 'signpost sentence' that links back to the key question that you must answer.
- Most students find the final paragraph the most difficult. Just repeating points you have already made earlier in the essay in a more simplified form will not bring you any extra credit. It is better to end your essay with your strongest and most convincing argument, which reinforces those you have made elsewhere. Supported by a brief quotation or reference to a relevant historian, this can be a very effective way of rounding off your essay.

# 2 Ambition and Reality: War Aims and the Peace Settlements of 1919–20

## POINTS TO CONSIDER

This chapter focuses initially on the question of how the war could be ended. It then looks at the Armistice Agreements of October and November 1918 and the five peace settlements of 1919–1920, which between them did much to recast Europe and the Middle East for the next 20 years. As you read through this chapter, you should consider first what each power hoped to achieve from the war and then go on to consider what in fact it gained at the Peace Conference. Also ask yourself whether, in reality, the Treaty of Versailles was as severe as the Germans claimed at the time.

## KEY DATES

| | | |
|---|---|---|
| 1914 | August | The First World War began |
| 1917 | April | America declared war on Germany |
| | November | Second Russian, or Bolshevik, Revolution |
| 1918 | 8 January | President Wilson announced 14 Points |
| | 3 March | Treaty of Brest-Litovsk signed |
| | 4 October | German Government seeks armistice on basis of the Fourteen Points |
| | 11 November | The German Armistice |
| 1919 | 18 January | Peace Conference opened at Paris |
| | 28 June | Treaty of Versailles signed with Germany |
| | 10 September | Treaty of St. Germain signed with Austria |
| | 27 November | Treaty of Neuilly signed with Bulgaria |
| 1920 | 10 January | Treaty of Versailles and League of Nations come into force |
| | 4 June | Treaty of Trianon signed with Hungary |
| | 10 August | Treaty of Sèvres signed with Turkey |

## 1 The Failure to Achieve a Negotiated Peace

> **KEY ISSUE** Why was it so difficult to end the war through negotiation?

Often wars are so much easier to start than end, and the First World war was no exception to this. Each government backed by its population was determined to secure victory. Britain wanted to destroy Germany's naval and colonial power and strengthen its position in the Middle East, while France aimed to weaken Germany permanently. In January 1917 Briand, the French premier, observed that:

1 In our eyes, Germany must no longer have a foot beyond the Rhine; the organisation of these territories, their neutrality and their temporary occupation must be considered in exchanges of opinion between the Allies. It is, however, important that France, being the most directly
5 concerned with the territorial status of this region, should have the casting vote in examining the solution of this serious question.

Germany's aims were the mirror image of France's. According to the September Programme, which was drawn up when Germany seemed to be about to win the war in September 1914, the Germans wished for:

1 Security for the German Reich in west and east for all imaginable time. For this purpose France must be so weakened as to make her revival as a Great Power impossible for all time. Russia must be thrust back as far as possible from Germany's eastern frontier and her domination
5 over non-Russian vassal peoples broken.

While the generals fought bloody wars of attrition, the diplomats on each side attempted to divide their enemies and achieve their government's aims in less costly ways. The Allies concentrated primarily on probing the possibilities of a separate peace with Germany's ally, Austria-Hungary, while Germany in turn tried similar tactics with Britain, France and Russia. Until 1917 the chances of a negotiated peace were minimal. The Allies were handicapped in their dealings with Vienna by their generous promises to Italy of Austrian territory in Istria and Dalmatia, which they had made to persuade Italy to enter the war on their side (see the map on page 32), when they signed the Treaty of London in 1915. On the other side, the scale of Germany's war aims, which entailed the German domination of Europe, proved a major obstacle to peace, as it was this very threat that the Allies were fighting.

Only in 1917 did a constellation of factors emerge that initially favoured the prospects for a negotiated peace. In March 1917 the first Russian revolution occurred, bringing to power a liberal regime, which, while still committed to fighting, was under intense internal pressure from the Bolsheviks (Communists) to make peace. The growing hostility of the Russian people to a war fought for territorial gains in turn influenced labour movements throughout Europe to agitate for a compromise peace. In July the German parliament actually passed a resolution calling for a 'peace of understanding'. In April the USA entered the war as an Associated Power, rather than as an ally. This ensured that the USA reserved its independence of action and could respond to peace initiatives as it thought fit. In Austria the aged and stubborn Emperor, Franz-Josef, died in November 1916, and the new Emperor, Charles, was determined to secure a separate peace. Finally in the summer of 1917 the French army was paralysed by a series of mutinies on the western front. Surely here were the ideal preconditions for a negotiated peace? Yet the peace initiatives launched by the Pope, the Austrians and the Socialist International Movement all failed because the gap between the belligerents was still too wide. Germany, encouraged by the rapid weakening of Russia, was determined to fight on, and its government increasingly fell under the influence of the generals, while Britain and France, now enormously strengthened by America's entry into the war, both decided that ultimately victory was still possible.

# 2 The Impact of the Bolshevik Revolution

> **KEY ISSUES** What was the impact of the Bolshevik Revolution on the course of the war, and why did Allied troops become involved in hostilities against the Bolsheviks?

In Russia the Bolsheviks overthrew the Provisional Government on 7 November 1917. The revolution was to be one of the defining events of twentieth-century history. Not only did it lead to a 3-year civil war in which the western powers became involved but it also gave the Germans their best chance of victory since August 1914. Lenin, the Bolshevik leader, although hoping that the revolution in Russia would trigger similar revolts throughout Europe, realised that if his regime was to survive he needed to make immediate peace with Germany. Thus on 3 March 1918 he signed the Treaty of Brest-Litovsk with Germany after announcing to the world that he supported a peace without annexations or reparations. The Germans were now free to transfer large numbers of men across to the western front to make one last attempt to break through before the American military build-up could become effective. On 21 March they launched a major offensive in the West. Simultaneously Germany tightened its grip on western Russia and in August forced Lenin both to grant independence to Georgia and to guarantee the punctual delivery of oil supplies to Germany. In response the Allies began to support the various anti-Bolshevik factions in the Russian civil war, in the hope that if they were victorious, Russia would rejoin the war against Russia. Once Germany was defeated in November 1918 the Allied forces were drawn deeper into the Russian civil war and their priority became the defeat of Bolshevism.

## 3 The Armistices of October and November 1918

KEY ISSUE   In what ways did the armistice agreements anticipate the coming peace treaties?

The great German offensive of March 1918 was halted in July, and on 29 September, after a series of military defeats in the west and the sudden request by their Bulgarian ally for a cease-fire in the east, the generals conceded defeat and advised the German Emperor to form a new constitutional government with the intention of negotiating an armistice with the USA. They calculated that only a democratic government could persuade President Wilson to grant generous conditions to Germany. Thus on 4 October the new more liberal German government asked Wilson for an immediate armistice on the basis of the Fourteen Points.

### THE FOURTEEN POINTS

America entered the war as a power 'associated' with, rather than allied with, the *Entente* and therefore felt free to formulate its own war aims independently of Britain and France. In January 1918 Wilson outlined America's war aims in the Fourteen Points, which consisted of the following proposals:

1 Open covenants [agreements], openly arrived at ... diplomacy shall always proceed frankly and in the public view.
2 Absolute freedom of navigation upon the seas, outside territorial waters ... .
3 The removal, so far as possible, of all economic barriers ... .
4 Adequate guarantees given and taken that national armaments will be reduced to the lowest point consistent with domestic safety.
5 A free, open-minded, and absolutely impartial adjustment of all colonial claims. ... the interests of the populations concerned must have equal weight with the equitable claims of the government whose title is to be determined.
6 The evacuation of all Russian territory ... .
7 Belgium, the whole world will agree, must be evacuated and restored, without any attempt to limit the sovereignty that it enjoys in common with all other free nations.
8 All French territory should be freed and the invaded portions restored, and the wrong done to France by Prussia in 1871 in the matter of Alsace Lorraine ... should be righted ...
9 A readjustment of the frontiers of Italy should be effected along clearly recognisable lines of nationality.

10 The peoples of Austria-Hungary, whose place among the nations we wish to see safeguarded and assured, should be accorded the freest opportunity of autonomous development.

11 Rumania, Serbia and Montenegro should be evacuated ... Serbia afforded free and secure access to the sea; and the relations of the several Balkan states to one another determined by friendly council along historically established lines of allegiance and nationality ...

12 The Turkish portions of the present Ottoman empire should be assured a secure sovereignty, but the other nationalities ... should be assured an absolutely unmolested opportunity of autonomous development, and the Dardanelles should be permanently open as a free passage to the ships and commerce of all nations ...

13 An independent Poland should be erected that should include the territories inhabited by indisputably Polish populations, which should be assured a free and secure access to the sea ...

14 A general association of nations must be formed under specific covenants for the purpose of political independence and territorial integrity to great and small states alike ...

Similar requests then came from Austria-Hungary and the Ottoman Empire. Germany's hopes of dividing its enemies were dashed when Wilson requested Allied military and naval experts to draft the details of the armistice agreements. Despite the presence of Colonel House, Wilson's personal representative, the Allies rapidly secured a series of tough terms, which anticipated the severity of the coming peace treaties:

• In the west the Germans were to evacuate all occupied territory, including Alsace-Lorraine and to withdraw beyond a 10-kilometre wide neutral zone to the east of the Rhine;
• Allied troops would then move in and occupy the west bank of the Rhine.
• In eastern Europe all German troops were similarly to be withdrawn from the occupied territories;
• The German navy was also to be interned in either a neutral or a British port.

Paralysed by mutinies and strikes, which forced the abdication of the Kaiser, the German government had little option but to accept the armistice on 11 November.

Austria-Hungary fared even worse. In the summer of 1918 America and the Allies had, in a desperate attempt to counter both German

## SOLDIER AND CIVILIAN.

MARSHAL FOCH (*to Messrs. CLEMENCEAU, WILSON and LLOYD GEORGE*). " IF YOU'RE GOING UP
THAT ROAD, GENTLEMEN, LOOK OUT FOR BOOBY-TRAPS."

Soldier and civilian, *Punch* cartoon, 23 October 1918.

successes in eastern Europe and a joint Austro-German decision to
create a permanent economic union, decided to abandon their
former policy of dealing with Austria-Hungary as a sovereign state.
Instead they recognised the right of its subject peoples, especially the

Czechs and the South Slavs or 'Yugoslavs' to independence. In Paris the exiled leaders of the Austrian Yugoslavs had already agreed to form a south Slav state (later to be called Yugoslavia), together with the Serbs, Croats and Slovenes. In October Wilson brushed aside attempts by Vienna to negotiate on behalf of its empire, and the Czechs and Yugoslavs seized the chance to declare their independence. On 1 November the Austro-Hungarian union was dissolved and 2 days later the former Imperial Austrian High Command negotiated an armistice with the Italians. In the meantime the Turkish armistice, which was largely negotiated by British officials to the exclusion of the French, was signed at Mudros on 30 October. It was a purely military agreement providing for the surrender of all the Turkish armed forces and the Allied occupation of key strategic points such as were necessary to control the Bosphorus and Dardanelles (see the map page 32).

# 4 Problems Facing the Peace-makers

> **KEY ISSUE** Why did the economic, political and social conditions of the time make it so much more difficult to negotiate a just and balanced peace settlements in Paris?

In January 1919 the statesmen of the victorious powers were confronted with a Europe in turmoil. The sudden and complete defeat of the Central Powers had made Europe vulnerable to the spread of Communism from Russia. Germany for much of the winter of 1918–19 seemed poised on the brink of revolution. With the disintegration of the Habsburg, Ottoman and Romanov empires there seemed to be no stable government anywhere east of the Rhine. In March when the Communist leader, Bela Kun, seized power in Hungary, it seemed to the Allied leaders that the door to the heart of Europe was now open to Communism.

Nor in eastern Europe and the Balkans did the end of hostilities between the Central Powers and the Allies lead to peace. At the railheads the Habsburg armies disintegrated, and Magyars, Poles, Czechs and Slavs fought with each other to seize weapons and munitions with which to equip their embryonic national armies and gain crucial territorial advantages in the struggle to set up new national states in the vacuum created by the collapse of Austria-Hungary and the defeat of Germany. In the Baltic Russian Bolshevik forces exploited the retreat of the Germans to occupy Lithuania and Latvia.

The fear of revolution was intensified by the influenza pandemic, which by the spring of 1919 had caused the deaths of millions of people, and by the near famine conditions in central and eastern Europe. The problems facing the statesmen in Paris were thus not only the negotiation of peace and the drawing up of new frontiers, but also the pressing need to avert economic chaos and famine. As one Allied official observed, 'There was a veritable race between peace and anarchy'.

The task of rebuilding a peaceful and prosperous Europe was made more difficult by the continued strength of nationalist feeling amongst the populations of the victorious powers. Nationalist opinion in Britain, America, France and Italy viewed the peace conference as the final phase of the war in which their leaders must ruthlessly consolidate the gains made on the battlefields and smash the enemy forever. Public opinion in the Allied nations and even in the USA turned decisively against a policy of conciliation. Everywhere the moderates lost ground. The greatest blow to the prospects for real peace in Europe were delivered when the Congressional elections in America in November 1918 gave the Republicans a majority. The Republicans were determined to campaign for a hard peace with Germany and simultaneously insist that America should become involved neither in guaranteeing it nor in financing any expensive schemes for European reconstruction.

# 5 Aims and Principles of the Victorious Great Powers

> **KEY ISSUES** What did the individual Allied and Associated Powers hope to achieve from the peace treaties? To what extent were these aims contradictory?

The peace negotiations at Paris are often interpreted as a struggle between the proponents of reconciliation, led by Wilson and Lloyd George, the British Prime Minister, and the ruthless advocates of a peace of revenge represented by Clemenceau, the French Prime Minister. The reality, however, was much more complicated.

## a) The USA: Wilson's Efforts to Implement the Fourteen Points

Wilson strongly believed that Germany needed to be punished for its part in starting the war and that it should be put on 'probation' before joining the League. In a speech at Omaha on 18 September 1919 he declared that the Treaty of Versailles:

1  seeks to punish one of the greatest wrongs ever done in history, the wrong which Germany sought to do to the world and to civilisation, and there ought to be no weak purpose with regard to punishment. She attempted an intolerable thing, and she must be made to pay for the
5  attempt.

Wilson was determined to ensure that the Fourteen Points would serve as a basis for the coming peace negotiations and anchor the Covenant (or constitution) of the League of Nations in the text of the peace treaties. He was convinced that then nearly all the serious difficulties at the peace conference would somehow disappear, as he assumed that this would automatically create a framework in which the other clauses of the treaties could be considered rationally. This was, however, to be a wildly optimistic assessment. There was broad general agreement amongst the victors to approve the creation of independent national states in eastern Europe and the Balkans and confine Turkey to its ethnic frontiers, all of which was anticipated by points 10–13. Points 7 and 8, covering the liberation of Belgium and the return of Alsace-Lorraine to France, had already been fulfilled at the start of the Armistice, while some of the other Points, the complete realisation of which would have created serious tensions between America and the Allies, were the subject of discrete compromise by Washington. Britain, for instance, was assured that point 2, which demanded the 'freedom of the seas', did not mean the immediate lifting of the blockade against Germany. The French and Belgians were promised American support for German reparations despite the absence of any such clause in the Fourteen Points, and Italy was promised the award of former Austrian territory up to the Brenner frontier even though this would include over 200,000 Germans. Wilson was also ready to compromise with Britain over the former German colonies and the Middle Eastern possessions of Turkey. These territories would be the ultimate responsibility of the new League of Nations but would be handed over as 'mandates' to the appropriate powers to administer. The British ambassador in Washington was specifically reassured by Wilson's adviser, Colonel House, that since Britain had pioneered the fairest colonial system in the world, it would therefore be an ideal mandatory power.

These concessions did not go far enough to turn the Fourteen Points into a practicable inter-Allied consensus for the coming peace negotiations. They failed to overcome imperialist rivalries between Britain and France in the Middle East or between America, Japan and Britain in the Far East. Nor, as will be seen, did they provide a solution to the rival claims in 1919–20 of Italy and the new 'kingdom of the Serbs, Croats and Slovenes' (which later became Yugoslavia) to Dalmatia.

## b) France's Priorities

More importantly they failed to impress the French Premier, Clemenceau, who was convinced that only an effective balance of power in Europe could contain Germany. He was painfully aware that France, with its reduced birthrate and a total number of casualties of 1.3 million dead and another 2.8 million wounded, faced a Germany that, as a consequence of the collapse of Austria-Hungary and Tsarist Russia, was potentially stronger than in 1914. He told the French parliament in December 1918:

1   There was an old system which seems condemned today and to which I do not hesitate to say that I remain to some extent faithful: nations organise their defence. It was very prosaic. They tried to have strong frontiers ... This system seems condemned today by the very high auth-
5   orities. Yet I believe that if this balance, which had been spontaneously produced during the war, had existed earlier: if, for example, England, America and Italy had agreed in saying that whoever attacked one of them had attacked the whole world, this war would never have taken place.

Clemenceau was anxious to enforce maximum disarmament on the Germans, to encourage a large independent Poland, and viable Czechoslovak and Yugoslav states, once it became clear that he could not rely on the restoration of Imperial Russia to restrain Germany, and to create an independent Rhineland state. He also intended to extract reparation payments from Germany. His main priority, how-ever, was to retain the wartime links with Britain and America and to continue inter-Allied financial and economic co-operation into the postwar years. He was ready to make considerable concessions to do this. For instance, in December 1918 in the Middle East he offered to cede Palestine and the Mosul oil fields to the British in the hope of gaining their support in Europe.

## c) Great Britain: A Satisfied Power?

In contrast to France, Britain, even before the great powers met in Paris, had already achieved many of its aims: the German fleet had surrendered, German trade rivalry was no longer a threat and Germany's colonial empire was liquidated, while the German armies in western Europe had been driven back into the Reich. Britain's ter-ritorial ambitions lay in the Middle East, not Europe. In January 1919 Lloyd George envisaged the preservation of a peaceful united Germany as a barrier against Bolshevism. Above all he wanted to avoid long-term British commitments on the continent of Europe and pre-vent the annexation of German minorities by the Poles or the French creating fresh areas of bitterness, which would sow the seeds of a new war. Inevitably, then, these objectives were fundamentally opposed to the French policy of securing definite guarantees against a German military revival either by negotiating a long-term Anglo-American military alliance or by a partial dismemberment of the German empire.

    The logic of British policy pointed in the direction of a peace of reconciliation rather than revenge, but in two key areas, reparations and the question of German war guilt, Britain adopted a more intransigent line. Lloyd George and Clemenceau agreed in December 1918 that the Kaiser should be tried by an international tribunal for war crimes. Under pressure from the Dominions, who also wanted a share of reparations, the British Delegation at Paris was authorised:

> to endeavour to secure from Germany the greatest possible indemnity she can pay consistently with the well being of the British Empire and the peace of the world without involving an army of occupation in Germany for its collection.

## d) Italy and Japan

The aims of both Japan and Italy were concentrated on maximising their war-time gains. Orlando, the Italian Prime Minister, was anxious to convince the voters that Italy had done well out of the war, and concentrated initially on attempting to hold the *Entente* to their promises made in the Treaty of London (see page 16), as well as demanding the port of Fiume in the Adriatic. Japan wanted recognition of its territorial gains. The Japanese government also pushed hard, but ultimately unsuccessfully, to have a racial equality clause included in the Covenant of the League of Nations. It hoped that this would protect Japanese immigrants in America.

## JAPAN'S GAINS IN THE WAR

The war had presented Japan with opportunities to increase its power in China and the Pacific region at a time when the energies of the European Powers were absorbed in Europe. The Japanese declared war on Germany on 23 August. The British had originally intended that the Japanese navy should merely help with convoy duties in the Pacific, but the Japanese refused to be relegated to a minor role and, much to the alarm of Britain, Australia and the USA, proceeded to seize German territory in the Chinese province of Shantung as well as the German Pacific islands. In January 1915 the Japanese pushed their luck further and presented China with the Twenty-One Demands, which not only included the recognition of the Japanese claims to Shantung and southern Manchuria but also proposed that the Chinese government should appoint Japanese advisers. This last demand would have turned China into a Japanese protectorate and was only dropped after strong British and American objections. However, the rest of the demands were accepted by China in May 1915 (see page 33).

# 6 The Organisation of the Paris Peace Conference

> **KEY ISSUES** How effective was the organisation of the Peace
> Conference? To what extent did the Council of Four emerge as
> the key decision-making body?

Compared to the Vienna Congress of 1814–15, the Paris Conference
was a showpiece of sophisticated organisation. The British delegation,
for instance, which was composed of 207 officials, as compared to a
mere 17 in 1814, had its own printing press, telephone lines to
London and the capitals of the Empire and a direct daily air link to
Croydon airfield, near London. Yet despite this impressive evidence
of outward efficiency, the Conference got off to a slow start and for
the first 2 months little progress was made towards a German settlement. The reasons for this were partly organisational and partly that
the Allied statesmen formed what Lloyd George called a 'Cabinet of
Nations', which could not ignore the pressing problems of immediate
post-war Europe. They had to consider the emergency consignments
of food to central and eastern Europe, set up the Supreme Economic
Council to deal with the financial and economic problems affecting
both occupied and unoccupied Germany and negotiate the easing
of the food blockade of Germany in exchange for the surrender of
the German merchant fleet. Above all they ceaselessly monitored the
progress of the civil war in Russia and weighed up the pros and cons
of Allied military intervention in it (see pages 47–8).

## a) The Council of Ten

When the Peace Conference opened on 18 January 1919 the delegates of 27 states attended, but in reality power lay with the 'big five':
Britain, France, Italy, Japan and the USA. Each, with the exception of
Japan, which to a great extent relied on its professional diplomats, was
at first represented by their wartime leaders in the Council of Ten
(two representatives per country). Neither Russia nor the defeated
enemy powers attended. Lloyd George and Wilson had both attempted
to secure Russian representation at Paris, but Allied efforts to negotiate a truce between the factions in the civil war failed when the
Whites refused to attend a conference on the island of Prinkipo in the
Sea of Mamara in February 1919. Right up to April the Allies were not
sure whether to follow the pattern of previous peace conferences and
plan for a preliminary peace with Germany and the other Central
Powers, which would only contain the disarmament terms and the
outlines of the territorial settlement; and then at a later date, when
passions had cooled, call an international congress to which the ex-

enemy states would be invited. Foch, the Supreme Allied Military Commander, was bitterly opposed to this scenario as he feared that the Germans would easily be able to exploit the tensions and rivalries between the Allies to gain major concessions.

Thus unsure in its own mind whether it was working on a preliminary or final treaty, the Council of Ten grappled with the intricate problems of peace-making. A total of 58 committees were set up to draft the clauses of not only the German treaty but also the treaties with Austria, Bulgaria, Hungary and Turkey. The Council's work was handicapped by the absence of any central co-ordinating body and consequently its different committees worked in isolation from each other, sometimes coming up with contradictory solutions.

## b) The Emergence of the Council of Four

It was not until 24 March that the organisation of the Conference was streamlined as a result of Lloyd George's controversial Fontainbleau Memorandum. Inspired by the fear that the Allies might drive Germany into the arms of the Bolsheviks, this urged major concessions to Berlin, and so raised important issues, which could only be resolved by secret discussions between Clemenceau, Lloyd George, Orlando and Wilson. This 'Council of Four' proved so effective that it became the key decision-making committee of the Conference. As most of the territorial committees had finished their reports, it was also decided to drop the idea of a preliminary peace and to proceed quickly to a final settlement with Germany, thereby abandoning the idea of a later congress and so minimising the opportunities for Germany to exploit inter-Allied differences at a time when the Allies were rapidly demobilising their armies.

Inevitably this decision had serious repercussions on the drafting of the treaty and possibly for the future peace of Europe. Harold Nicolson, a member of the British delegation at Paris, argued in 1933 that

1  Many paragraphs of the Treaty, and especially in the economic section, were in fact inserted as 'maximum statements' such as would provide some area of concession to Germany at the eventual congress. This congress never materialised: the last weeks flew past us in a hysterical
5  nightmare; and these 'maximum statements' remained unmodified and were eventually imposed by ultimatum.

On the other hand, it is arguable that such were the problems the Allied statesmen faced in 1919 that, as Max Beloff has observed, it is surprising 'not that the treaties were imperfect but that they were concluded at all'.[1]

# 7 The Settlement with Germany

> **KEY ISSUES** How much of a compromise between America, France and Britain was the Treaty of Versailles? To what extent was it a harsh treaty?

All peace settlements are to a greater or lesser extent the result of compromises between the negotiating powers. Versailles was no exception. Its key clauses were the result of fiercely negotiated agreements, which were often only reached when the conference appeared to be on the brink of collapse. The first 26 articles (which appeared in all the other treaties as well) contained the Covenant of the League of Nations (see pages 78–80) and were agreed unanimously once Wilson had met French objections by initially excluding Germany from the League.

## a) German War Guilt

Despite some American and Italian reservations, which were eventually overcome by Lloyd George and Clemenceau, about the legality of demanding the surrender of the Kaiser and other German leaders for trial for committing acts against 'international morality',[2] there was universal agreement amongst the victorious powers that Germany was guilty of having started the war. It was this principle of war guilt, which was to provide the moral justification for the reparation clauses of the Treaty that was stressed in Article 231 of the Treaty:

1  The Allied and Associated Governments affirm and Germany accepts
   the responsibility of Germany and her allies for causing all the loss and
   damage to which the Allied and Associated Governments and their
   nationals have been subjected as a consequence of the war imposed up
5  them by the aggression of Germany and her allies.

## b) Reparations

Although there was general agreement that Germany should pay an indemnity to the victors, there was considerable debate about the amount it should pay, the nature of the damage deserving compensation and how Germany could raise such large sums of money without harming the Allied economies. Essentially the major issue behind the Allied demands was the compelling need to cover the costs of financing the war. Britain had covered one-third of its war expenditure through taxation, France just one-sixth. At a time of severe social unrest no Allied country could easily face the prospect of financing debt repayments by huge tax increases and savage cuts in expenditure. Initially it was hoped that America could be persuaded to continue wartime inter-Allied economic cooperation and above all cancel the repayment of Allied war debts, but by the end of 1918 it was obvious that this was not going to happen, as Wilson dissolved all the agencies for inter-Allied co-operation in Washington. Without American participation the British Treasury was reluctant to continue its wartime cooperation with the French Finance Ministry and in March 1919 all further financial assistance from Britain to France was stopped. France had no option therefore but to seek financial reparation from Germany. The French appeared to have operated on two levels. The French finance minister, Louis Klotz, backed by the press and the Chamber of Deputies, urged a policy of maximum claims, and coined the slogan that 'Germany will pay' (for everything). Behind the scenes, however, Loucheur, the Minister for Reconstruction, pursued a more subtle policy and informed the Germans that such was the need of the French economy for an immediate injection of cash that his government would settle for a more moderate sum, which the Germans would be able to raise quickly through the sale of bonds on the world's financial markets. The German government, however, suspected that these overtures were merely a means of dividing Germany from America, which was seen in Berlin as the country potentially most sympathetic to the German cause. America's reparation policy was certainly more moderate than either Britain's or France's as it recommended that a modest fixed sum should be written into the Treaty.

The British delegation consistently maximised their country's reparation claims on Germany. Some historians explain this in terms of the pressure exerted on the government by the electorate. On the other hand, Lloyd George himself claimed that 'the imposition of a high indemnity ... would prevent the Germans spending money on an army'.[3] It was arguable that a high indemnity would also ensure that there would be money left over for Britain and the Dominions after France and Belgium had claimed their share. To safeguard Britain's percentage of reparations, the Imperial War Cabinet urged that the cost of war pensions should be included in the reparation bill. By threatening to walk out of the Conference, Lloyd George then forced the Council of Four to support his arguments. The British pension claims made it even more difficult for the Allied financial experts to agree on an overall figure for reparations. Consequently, at the end of April, it was agreed that the Reparation Commission should be set up to assess in detail by 1 May 1921 what the German economy could afford. In the meantime, the Germans would make an interim payment of 20 milliard (or American billion) gold marks and raise a further 60 milliard through the sale of bonds. It was not until December 1919 that Britain and France agreed on the ratio 25:55 respectively as the percentage of the total reparations, which each power should eventually receive. Belgium was the only power to be awarded full compensation for its losses and priority in payment of the first sums due from Germany, largely because it too threatened to withdraw from the Conference in May at a time when Italy had already walked out and the Japanese were also threatening to do so (see pages 33, 37–8).

## c) German Disarmament

As with reparations, the Allied and Associated nations agreed on the necessity for German disarmament, but there were differences in emphasis. The British and Americans wished to destroy in Germany the tradition of conscription, which they regarded as 'the taproot of militarism',[4] while Foch, more wisely as it turned out, feared that a professional army would become a tightly organised nucleus which would be capable of quick expansion when the opportunity arose. Foch was overruled and the Council of Ten accepted in March proposals for the creation of inter-Allied commissions to monitor the pace of German disarmament, the abolition of the General Staff, the creation of a regular army of 100,000 men, the dissolution of the air-force and the reduction of the navy to a handful of ships.

## d) The Territorial Settlement

It was accepted, even by the many Germans, that the predominantly Danish northern Schleswig, annexed by Bismarck in 1866, should be returned to the Danes. There was therefore general agreement that a plebiscite should be held to determine the size of the area to be handed back. The former German territories of Eupen and Malmedy, together with Moresnet, which before 1914 had been administered jointly by Germany and Belgium, were ceded to Belgium, and the neutrality of the Grand Duchy of Luxemburg was confirmed.

The French proposals for the future of the Saar proved more controversial. Clemenceau insisted on the restoration to France of that part of the Saar, which was given to Prussia in 1814. He also aimed to detach the mineral and industrial basin to the north, which had never been French and place it under an independent non-German administration. Finally he demanded full French ownership of the Saar coalmines to compensate for the destruction of the pits in Northern France by the Germans. Wilson immediately perceived that here was a clash between the national interests of France and the principle of self-determination as enshrined in the Fourteen Points. While he was ready to agree to French access to the coalmines until the production of their own mines had been restored, he vetoed outright other demands. To save the Conference from breaking down Lloyd George persuaded Wilson and Clemenceau to accept a compromise whereby the mines would be transferred to French ownership, while the actual government of the Saar would be entrusted to the League. After 15 years the people would have the right to decide in a plebiscite whether they wished to return to German rule.

Over the future of the Rhineland there was an equally bitter clash between Britain and France. The British had no ambitions on the Rhine, but to the French the occupation of the Rhine was a unique opportunity to weaken Germany permanently by detaching the whole area from it. The British feared that not only would this create a new area of tension between France and Germany but that it would tilt the balance of power in Europe decisively towards France. Only after heated and often bitter arguments was a compromise at last reached. Clemenceau agreed to limit the Allied occupation of the Rhineland to a 15-year period in return for an Anglo-American treaty guaranteeing France against a new German attack. The Rhineland would be divided into three zones, which would be evacuated after 5, 10 and 15 years. Thereafter the Rhineland would be a demilitarised zone barred to German troops, but under German administration. Lloyd George was unwilling to accept even this length of occupation and right up to the signature of the Treaty he sought to evade the commitment.

Anglo-French disagreements again dominated negotiations on Germany's eastern frontiers. The Commission on Polish Affairs recommended on 12 March that Danzig, Marienwerder and Upper Silesia should all be included in the new Polish state and that the future of Allenstein should be decided by plebiscite. Lloyd George vigorously opposed the inclusion of Danzig and Marienwerder as he feared the long-term resentment of the local and predominantly German-speaking population and dreaded that an embittered Germany might turn to Bolshevik Russia for help. By threatening to withdraw from the Anglo-American guarantee pact, he forced Clemenceau to agree to the holding of a plebiscite in Marienwerder and the establishment of a free and autonomous city of Danzig to be linked with Poland through a customs union and presided over by a High Commissioner appointed by the League of Nations.

## e) German Colonies

President Wilson insisted that the League should also have ultimate control over the former German colonies. This was accepted only reluctantly by the British Dominions of New Zealand, Australia and South Africa, each arguing that the outright annexation by themselves of, respectively, the South Pacific islands, Samoa and South West Africa was vital for Imperial security. In May agreement was reached on the division of the German colonies. Britain, France and South Africa were allocated most of the former German colonial empire in Africa, while Australia, New Zealand and Japan secured the mandates for the scattered German possessions in the Pacific. Italy was awarded control of the Juba valley in East Africa, and a few minor territorial adjustments were made to its Libyan frontier with Algeria. Essentially Britain, the Dominions and France had secured what they

Central Europe after the Peace Settlements, 1919–23.

wanted, despite paying lip-service to the League by agreeing to mandate status for the former German colonies.

A more serious clash arose between Japan and America. The
Japanese were determined to hold on to the ex-German leasehold territory of Kiaochow in Shantung in China. The Chinese government,
however, on the strength of its declaration of war against Germany in
1917, argued that all former German rights should automatically

revert to the Chinese state, despite the fact that in 1915 it had agreed to recognise Japanese rights in Shantung. Wilson was anxious to block the growth of Japanese influence in the Pacific and supported China, but Lloyd George and Clemenceau, wanting to protect their own rights in China, backed Japan. Wilson, already locked in conflict with the Italians over their claims to Fiume (see pages 37–8) and facing Japanese threats to boycott the Conference and sign a separate peace with Germany, had no option but to concede. It is arguable that this humiliating defeat did much to turn the American Senate against the treaty of Versailles.

## f) The German Reaction

While the Allies were working on the Treaty, the German government could only prepare for the time when it would be summoned to Paris to receive the draft treaty. Optimistically in what one German intellectual, Ernst Troeltsch, called 'the dreamland of the armistice period',[5] Berlin hoped that it would be able to protect Germany from excessive reparation claims and so keep the way open for a rapid economic recovery.

On 7 May the draft peace terms were at last presented to the Germans, who were given a mere 15 days to draw up their reply. The German government bitterly criticised the Treaty on the basis that it did not conform to the Fourteen Points and demanded significant concessions:

- immediate membership of the League of Nations;
- a guarantee that Austria and the ethnic Germans in the Sudetenland, which was a part of the new Czechoslovak state, should have the chance to decide whether they wished to join Germany;
- and the setting up of a neutral commission to examine the war guilt question.

These demands, which if met would have strengthened Germany's position in central Europe, were rejected outright by the Allied and Associated Powers, but nevertheless some ground was conceded. Lloyd George, fearful that the Germans might reject the treaty, persuaded the French to agree to a plebiscite in Upper Silesia. He failed to limit the Rhineland occupation to 5 years, but did manage to secure the vague assurance, which later became Article 431 of the Treaty, 'that once Germany had given concrete evidence of her willingness to fulfil her obligations', the Allied and Associated Powers would consider 'an earlier termination of the period of occupation'.[6]

On 16 June the Germans were handed the final version of the Treaty incorporating these concessions. Not surprisingly, given the depth of opposition to it amongst the German people, it triggered a political crisis splitting the Cabinet and leading to the resignation of the Chancellor. Yet in view of its own military weakness, the Berlin

THE RECKONING.

PAN-GERMAN. "MONSTROUS, I CALL IT. WHY, IT'S FULLY A QUARTER OF WHAT *WE* SHOULD HAVE MADE *THEM* PAY, IF *WE'D* WON."

The Reckoning. *Punch* Cartoon, 23 April 1919.

Government had little option but to accept the Treaty, although it made very clear that it was acting under duress:

> Surrendering to superior force but without retracting its opinion regarding the unheard of injustice of the peace conditions, the Government of the German Republic therefore declares its readiness to accept and sign the peace conditions imposed by the Allied and Associated Governments.

## g) The Signature of the Treaty

On 28 June 1919 the Treaty was signed in the Hall of Mirrors at Versailles, where in 1871 the German Empire had been proclaimed. By January 1920 it had been ratified by all the signatory powers with the important exception of America. In Washington crucial amendments had been put forward by a coalition of isolationists, led by senators Lodge and Borah, rejecting the Shantung settlement and seriously modifying the Covenant of the League. The isolationists objected to the right of the British Dominions to vote as separate members of the League and were determined to subject America's obligation to defend the independence of fellow League members from aggression to strict control by Congress. They also proposed that Congress should be empowered to veto American participation in any League initiative that clashed with America's traditional policy, laid down in 1823 in the Monroe Doctrine, of excluding foreign intervention from both north and south America. Wilson felt that these amendments would paralyse the League and so refused to accept them. He failed twice to secure the necessary two-thirds majority in the Senate. It was a major defeat for Wilson, and the consequences for Europe were serious. Without American ratification the Anglo-American military guarantee of France lapsed and the burden of carrying out the Treaty of Versailles was mainly to fall upon Britain and France (see Chapter 3).

# 8 The South Eastern European Settlements

> **KEY ISSUES**  What were the main terms of the Treaties of St Germain, Neuilly and the Trianon? How effectively did they create new nation states?

After the ceremony at Versailles the Allied leaders returned home, leaving their officials to draft the treaties with Germany's former allies. The outlines of a settlement in eastern Europe and the Balkans were already clear: Austria-Hungary and the Tsarist Russian empire had collapsed, the Poles and Czechs had declared their independence and the South Slavs had decided to federate with Serbia to form what was later to be called Yugoslavia. The bewildering diversity of races in the Balkans, which were in no way concentrated in easily definable areas, would ensure that however the great powers drew the frontiers the final settlement would be full of contradictions. The three defeated powers, Austria and Hungary (both treated as the heirs to the former Habsburg Empire) and Bulgaria, all had to pay reparations, disarm and submit to the humiliation of a war guilt clause. The basis of the settlement in south central Europe and the Balkans was the creation of the new Czecho-Slovak state and Serbo-Croat-Slovene state, or Yugoslavia.

## a) The Treaty of St Germain, 10 September 1919

The Treaty of St Germain split up the diverse territories, which before the war had been part of Austria:

- Italy was awarded South Tyrol, despite the existence there of some 230,000 ethnic Germans.

- Bohemia and Moravia were ceded to Czechoslovakia. Any second thoughts that the British or Americans had about handing over to the Czechs the 3 million Germans who made up nearly a third of the population of these provinces, were quickly stifled by French opposition. The French wanted a potential ally against Germany to be strengthened by a defensible frontier and the possession of the Skoda munitions works in Pilsen, both of which entailed the forcible integration of large German minorities into Czechoslovakia. The British and Americans were also reassured by the promises of Eduard Benes, the Czech representative at Paris, that his government would make Czechoslovakia a racially harmonious federal republic like Switzerland.
- Slovenia, Bosnia-Herzegovina and Dalmatia were handed over to Yugoslavia.
- Galicia and Bukovina were ceded respectively to Poland and Romania.
- Only in Carinthia, where the population consisted of German-speaking Slovenes who did not want to join Yugoslavia, did the great powers consent to a plebiscite. This resulted in 1920 in that area remaining Austrian.
- To avoid the dangers of an Austrian union with Germany, Article 88 (which was identical with Article 80 in the Treaty of Versailles) stated that only the Council of the League of Nations was empowered to sanction a change in Austria's status as an independent state. Effectively this meant that France, as a permanent member of the Council, could veto any proposed change.

## b) The Treaty of Trianon, 4 June 1920

Of all the defeated powers in 1919 it is arguable that Hungary suffered the most severely. By the Treaty of Trianon it lost over two-thirds of its territory and 41.6% of its population. In an age of nationalism it was particularly vulnerable to partition, as essentially only the heartlands of Hungary, the great Central Plain, were Magyar (ethnic Hungarian). Its fate was sealed, when, in November 1918 Serb, Czech and Romanian troops all occupied the regions they claimed. The completion of the treaty was delayed by Bela Kun's coup in March (see page 21). He succeeded in driving out the Czechs from eastern Slovakia, but was himself defeated by Romanian troops in August. Negotiations with the new Hungarian government were resumed in January 1920 and concluded in June. Most of the German-speaking area in the west of the former Hungarian state was ceded to Austria, the Slovakian and Ruthenian regions in the north went to Czechoslovakia, the east to Romania and the south to Yugoslavia. The Treaty of Trianon was justified by the Allies according to the principle of self-determination, but in the context of Hungary this was a principle almost impossible to realise. C.A. Macartney, an expert on Hungary and the successor states, observed in 1937:

1    ... the ethical line was practically nowhere clear cut ... long centuries of interpenetration, assimilation, migration and internal colonisation had left in many places a belt of mixed and often indeterminate population where each national group merged into the next, while there were
5    innumerable islands of one nationality set in seas of another, ranging in size from the half-million of Magyar speaking Szekely in Transylvania through many inter-determinate groups of fifty or a hundred thousand down to communities of a single village or less ... No frontier could be drawn which did not leave national minorities on at least one side of it.

Wherever there was a clash of interests between Hungary and the successor states or Romania, the Allies ensured that the decision went against Hungary.

## c) The Treaty of Neuilly, 27 November 1919

This same principle operated in the negotiations leading up to the Treaty of Neuilly with Bulgaria, which was signed on November 1919. Essentially Britain and France regarded Bulgaria as the 'Balkan Prussia' which needed to be restrained. They were determined, despite reservations from Italy and America, to reward their allies, Romania, Greece and Serbia (now part of Yugoslavia) at its expense. Thus southern Dobruja, with a mere 7000 Romanians out of a total population of 250,000, was ceded to Romania and western Thrace was given to Greece.

## d) Fiume, Istria and Dalmatia and the Treaty of Rapallo, November 1920

These postwar settlements were accompanied by bitter quarrels between the Allied powers and Associated powers. The most serious clash of opinions took place between Italy and America over Italian claims to Fiume, Istria and Dalmatia which Britain and France had recognised in the Treaty of London of 1915. Orlando and Sonnino were desperate to prove to their electorate that Italy was not a 'proletarian nation' which could be dictated to by the great powers, and insisted on their right to annex both Albania and the port of Fiume in which, it could be argued, there was a bare majority of ethnic Italians if the Croat suburb of Susak was conveniently left out of the picture. The Italian annexation of Fiume would have the added bonus of denying Yugoslavia its only effective port in the Adriatic, thereby strengthening Italy's economic grip on the region. Agreement could have been achieved, especially as Orlando was ready in April 1919 to accept Fiume as a compromise for giving up Italian claims on Dalmatia; but Wilson made the major political mistake of vetoing this option publicly in a statement in the French press. After compromising over the Saar and Shantung (see pages 30, 32–3), Wilson was stubbornly determined to make a stand on the

Fourteen Points in the Adriatic. Orlando and Sonnino walked out of the Peace Conference in protest and did not return until 9 May.

Orlando's resignation and his replacement by Nitti in June opened the way up for secret negotiations in Paris, but the lynching of nine French troops in Fiume by an Italian mob in July and then the seizure of the city in September by the Italian nationalist poet d'Annunzio merely prolonged the crisis. An agreement was reached in 1920 once the Yugoslavs realised that Wilson lacked the domestic support to interfere in the details of the Balkan settlements and when the Italian government, which was anxious to concentrate on Italy's pressing social and economic problems, showed its willingness to compromise by ending its wartime occupation of southern Albania. In November 1920 Yugoslavia and Italy signed the Treaty of Rapallo. Istria was partitioned between the two powers, Fiume became a self-governing free city and the rest of Dalmatia went to Yugoslavia. In December Italian troops cleared d'Annunzio out of Fiume, although in late 1923 Mussolini reoccupied it.

# 9 The Settlement with Turkey, 1919–23

> **KEY ISSUES** What were the main terms of the Treaty? To what extent was it so harsh that it was bound to provoke a backlash?

The Treaty of Sèvres was another Anglo-French compromise. Lloyd George hoped drastically to weaken Turkey by depriving it not only of Constantinople and of the control of the Straits, but also by forcing it to surrender all territories where arguably there was no ethnic Turkish majority. He now envisaged Greece rather than Italy (see page 59) as filling the vacuum left by the collapse of Turkish power and, in effect, becoming the agent of the British Empire in the eastern Mediterranean. The French, on the other hand, concerned to protect their prewar investments in Turkey, wished to preserve a viable Turkish state. Above all, they wanted the Turkish government to remain in Constantinople where it would be more vulnerable to French pressure.

The end product of this Anglo-French compromise was a harsh and humiliating treaty. Constantinople remained Turkish, but Thrace and most of the European coastline of the Sea of Marmara and the Dardanelles were to go to Greece (see maps, pages 32 and 39). In the Smyrna region the Greeks were also given responsibility for internal administration and defence, while an Armenian state was to be set up with access across Turkish territory to the Black Sea. The Straits were to be controlled by an international commission, and an Allied financial committee was to have the right to inspect Turkey's finances. By a separate agreement zones were also awarded to France and Italy in southern Turkey.

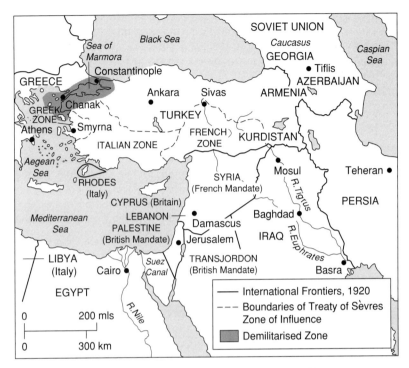

The Near and Middle East after the Treaty of Sèvres.

# 10 Assessment

> **KEY ISSUES** Can the peace settlements of 1919–20 be defended?
> To what extent did they contain the seeds of their own
> destruction?

The peace treaties of 1919–20 were seen by some contemporaries as
a triumph of democracy, the rule of law, self-determination and collective security against militarism, and yet by others as a hypocritical
act of vengeance and economic ignorance. The treaties contained a
unique combination of idealism and morality with old-fashioned
power politics. At past peace conferences there had been the assumption by both victors and the defeated that eventually the territorial
settlement would be modified in a new war. In the First World War
the slaughter had been so terrible that public opinion in Europe
wanted future conflict prevented, whether by a severe peace permanently weakening the Central Powers or by more liberal measures
overseen by the League of Nations. Consequently the treaties of
1919–20 were judged by almost impossibly high standards.

Increasingly, as a result of the devastating criticisms in *The Economic Consequences of the Peace*, which was a brilliant analysis of the Versailles Treaty written in 1919 by John Maynard Keynes, an economist, who had been a member of the British delegation in Paris, public opinion in Britain and America began to turn against the peace. Keynes summarised his arguments as follows:

> 1 ... the treaty ignores the economic solidarity of Europe and by aiming
> at the destruction of the economic life of Germany it threatens the
> health and prosperity of the Allies themselves.
> 2 ... the German economic system as it existed before depended on ...
> 5   i) Overseas commerce as represented by her Mercantile marine
> [most of which had to be handed over to the Allies], her colonies, her
> foreign investments, her exports ... ii) The exploitation of her coal
> and iron and the industries built upon them ... The Treaty aims at the
> systematic destruction of [this system].

To the Germans Keynes' arguments seemed to provide the final proof that the Allies led by Clemenceau were out to destroy their country, yet viewed from the perspective of 1945 the Treaty of Versailles does not appear as harsh as it did in 1919. Germany was still potentially a great power. It is arguable, too, that it was as much the hostility of the German industrialists to reparations, and the refusal of the American government to assist France financially, as the greed of the Allies that rendered the payment of reparations so difficult to achieve.

Unlike the Vienna settlement, the peace treaties failed to create a new balance of power in Europe. The Habsburg Empire was replaced by several small unstable states. Italy felt cheated by the Peace and was to remain a revisionist power in the Mediterranean and the Adriatic. Even Britain and France, which gained most from Versailles, in fact secured only short-term advantages as they were too divided by mutual suspicions to implement the treaties in the crucial postwar years. Essentially the real weakness of the settlements of 1919–20 was that America, which had played such a part in negotiating them, was prevented by the vote in the Senate from helping to carry them out. One American historian, Paul Birdsall, argued that

> the defection of the United States destroyed the Anglo-American pre-
> ponderance which above all could have stabilised Europe. It impaired
> the authority and prestige of the League at its birth and it precipitated
> an Anglo-French duel which reduced Europe to the chaos from which
> 5 Hitler emerged to produce new chaos ...

## References

1  M. Beloff, *Britain's Liberal Empire, 1897–1921* (London, Methuen, 1969), p. 279.
2  Quoted from Article 227 of the Treaty of Versailles.
3  Quoted in M. Trachtenberg, *Reparation in World Politics* (New York, Columbia University Press, 1980), p. 48.

4  General Smuts quoted in L. Jaffe, *The Decision to Disarm Germany* (London, Allen and Unwin, 1985), p. 189.
5  Quoted in E. Kolb, *The Weimar Republic* (London, Routledge, 2nd edition, 1990), p. 30.
6  Quoted in D. Williamson, *The British in Germany* (Oxford, Berg, 1991), p. 23.

## Summary Diagram

### The Peace Settlements, 1919–23

| Problems | Principles |
|---|---|
| 1 Revolutionary condition of Europe<br>2 Russian civil war<br>3 Diverging Allied aims<br>4 Competing nationalisms<br>5 Desire for revenge<br>6 Hunger, disease, economic chaos<br>7 Allied lack of military strength as a result of demobilisation | 1 Independence for subject nations<br>2 International rule of law through the League of Nations<br>3 Disarmament and reparation from defeated powers<br>4 Determination to prove German war guilt<br>5 Selective (?) application of 14 points |

### The Versailles Settlement, June 1919

| Territorial changes | Reparations | Disarmament | League of Nations |
|---|---|---|---|
| Independent Poland<br><br>Plebiscites in Upper Silesia, Schleswig and West Prussia<br><br>Alsace-Lorraine to France<br><br>Saar administered by League of Nations<br><br>Germany loses colonies and foreign investments | Reparation Commission fixes amount of 132 milliard gold marks in May 1921<br><br>Prolonged struggle to force Germany to pay, 1921–3<br><br>France occupies Ruhr in Jan 1923<br><br>Dawes Commission Jan 1924 | Abolition of conscription<br><br>Regular German army of 100,000<br><br>Very small fleet<br><br>Allied Control Commissions in Germany until 1927<br><br>Rhineland occupied for 15 years | Collective security<br><br>New principle of mandates<br><br>Weakened by absence of USA<br><br>Germany and defeated powers initially excluded |

### The Eastern European, Balkan and Near East Peace Settlements

| St Germain | Trianon | Neuilly | Sèvres | Riga |
|---|---|---|---|---|
| Czechoslovakia set up<br><br>Slovenia, Bosnia, Dalmatia to Yugoslavia<br><br>Istria, Trieste and S. Tyrol to Italy<br><br>Galicia to Poland<br><br>Austria not to integrate with Germany | Hungary loses 2/3 of its pre-war territory to Austria, Czechoslovakia and Romania | Bulgaria loses territory to Greece, Romania and Yugoslavia | Turks cede Middle East empire; Greeks gain Thrace; Straits controlled by Allies<br><br>Revised at Lausanne, 1923: Greeks expelled, Constantinople back to Turkey | Russia defeated by Poland, August 1920<br><br>Poland's eastern frontiers fixed by Treaty of Riga, March 1921 |

## Working on Chapter 2

In making notes on this chapter you should concentrate first of all on the background to the peace conference. Ask yourself why a genuine peace had not been negotiated earlier. Did Germany's defeat thus ensure that Versailles would be a dictated peace? When you move on to analyse the peace treaties ask yourself three key questions: 1) What were the aims of the peace-makers? 2) What political, social and economic conditions made the negotiation of treaties particularly difficult? Look in particular at events in Russia and Central Europe. 3) To what extent were the treaties a compromise between the conflicting aims of the great powers? Finally when you have completed these tasks, try to assess how effective the peace settlements were, even though this is an ongoing question throughout the book.

## Answering structured and essay questions on Chapter 2

In this chapter you have looked first at the aims of all the belligerent powers during the war and then at the negotiation and contents of the five separate peace treaties, which concluded the war against the Central Powers. It is vital for you to have a good basic knowledge of the peace treaties so that you can assess how they affected Europe and the world in the subsequent interwar period. Look at the following structured questions:

1 **a)** What did Great Britain, France and the USA hope to gain from victory over the Central Powers?
  **b)** To what extent were the objectives of these powers contradictory?
2 **a)** Outline the key policies adopted by the Allied and Associated Powers for weakening Germany in the Treaty of Versailles.
  **b)** To what extent was the Treaty of Versailles a 'dictated' and harsh peace?

Both 1a) and 2a) are straightforward questions, which are testing your factual knowledge. Questions 1b) and 2b) are more difficult because you have to analyse and make a judgement based on the facts. In 1b) you have to compare the war aims of three great powers. The wrong way to do this is to write a paragraph on the objectives of each power and to leave it to the examiner to draw the right conclusions. You need, instead, to adopt a thematic approach. One paragraph, for instance, might look at colonial gains, noting, particularly, Anglo-French rivalry in the Middle East, while stressing that the Americans proposed creating mandates rather than new colonies, which would be administered by a particular power on behalf of the new League of Nations. In other paragraphs you will have to deal with the core questions of Germany and the successor states to the Austro-Hungarian Empire. Again, it is vital to compare the relevant policies of Britain, France and the USA point by point. In dealing with their intentions towards Germany you will, of course, need to give a detailed analysis of each power's objectives, but it is a good idea to begin the section on Germany, for example, with a 'signpost sentence', such as: 'While Britain and US essentially wanted a prosperous but peaceful Germany, which would help the global economy recover, the French were more concerned with permanently weakening her'. This signals to the examiner that you intend to answer the question throughout the essay rather than leaving comparisons to the very end. The expression 'to what extent' is very popular with examiners and means in effect 'how far or 'how much', and is asking you to exercise your judgement. In Question 2b), for instance, there is obviously a considerable body of evidence to draw on, yet how harsh was Versailles when compared to the Treaty of Brest-Litovsk and Germany's fate in 1945, which ended in complete occupation and eventual partition?

Essay questions on the treaties usually fall into two main groups: the more detailed questions requiring a critical analysis of their contents, and then those that are more concerned with their longer-term consequences. In this last category examiners often expect you to trace the impact of the treaties up to 1930 or even 1939. Thus a discussion of this type of question is best left until you have read and worked on the next chapter. Study the following titles that are all specific questions on the treaties:

**1**  'Neither a peace of revenge nor a peace of reconciliation.' Was this the fatal weakness in the Treaty of Versailles?
**2**  Discuss the view that the Versailles settlement was an unsatisfactory compromise between hopes for reconciliation and a desire to punish Germany.
**3**  'Vicious and short-sighted.' How correct is this assessment of the peace settlements of 1919–20?
**4**  Were the postwar treaties a defeat for Wilsonian liberalism?

Only one of these, number 4, is set in the form of a simple question. In the others the examiner employs a popular technique, of putting forward an interpretation and asking you to assess it. You must be careful when answering this type of question not to fall into the trap of giving a long narrative account of the contents of the Treaty. You do not, of course, have to agree with the examiner. You will, as always, need to be analytical in your approach and to show, for instance in Questions 1 and 2, that almost every section of Versailles was in fact a compromise between the conflicting demands of the Allies and America. You should ask yourself whether this was necessarily a 'fatal weakness'. After all, diplomacy cannot usually succeed without compromise. Perhaps the refusal of America to ratify the Treaty was the real undoing of Versailles?

The next two questions are more general and require you to consider all the peace settlements. Always avoid both excessive narrative and too much detail if you wish to finish the question in time! The best way to do this is to answer the questions thematically. For instance, you could consider the treatment of the nationality problem by all the treaties in one section of the essay and then go on and analyse the military, economic, imperialist or annexationist aims in other sections. In Question 4 you would also need to understand the implications of the Fourteen Points as well as knowing the details of Wilsonian diplomacy in Paris. As historical issues are so often complex and contradictory, you may well wish to question whether such statements as 'vicious and short-sighted' can be applied to all aspects of the peace treaties.

## Source-based questions on Chapter 2

The first and most essential skill in dealing with source-based questions is to make sure that you understand the context and background of the documents and technical terms used in them.

1 **The Fourteen Points**
   Carefully read the extract from the Fourteen Points on pages 18 and 19 and answer the following questions:
   **a)** Explain the meaning of the second point. Against whom was it directed? (*3 marks*)
   **b)** What are the implications of the tenth point for the continued existence of Austria-Hungary? In answering this consider whether any of the other points are relevant. (*5 marks*)
   **c)** Read the Fourteen Points through carefully. In what way do they help explain why the Germans hoped to negotiate an armistice with Wilson rather than with the Allies? Explain your answer fully and also use your own knowledge (*7 marks*)

2 **French war aims and policy during the Peace Conference**
   Read carefully the extract from Briand's statement on page 16 (Source A) and from Clemenceau's speech on page 24 (Source B). Answer the following questions:
   **a)** **i** Study Souce A.
      From this source and your own knowledge explain what Briand means when he says Germany must no longer have a foot beyond the Rhine (line 1) (*2 marks*)
      **ii** Study Source B.
      What does Clemenceau mean by the 'balance ... spontaneously produced during the war' (lines 5–6)? (*3 marks*)
   **b)** Study both sources.
      **i** How useful are they as a guide to French policy at the Paris Peace Conference? (*10 marks*)
      **ii** Using both sources and your own knowledge, explain why a wide gap developed between British and French policies during the Paris Peace Conference. (*15 marks*)

**3   The German war guilt question**
Read carefully the extracts from the September Programme on page 16 (Source A), Wilson's speech at Omaha on page 22 (Source B), Article 231 of the Treaty of Versailles on page 28 (Source C), the Berlin government's declaration in June on page 34 (Source D). Also look at the cartoon on page 34 (Source E). Answer the following questions:

**a)**   Study Source D.
Explain the meaning of 'Surrendering to superior force ... without retracting its opinion' (line 1). (*2 marks*)

**b)**   Study Sources B and C
How do these sources seek to emphasise Germany's war guilt? Why was this so important for the Allies and America? (*6 marks*)

**c)**   Study Source E.
Assess the value of the cartoon to an historian studying the question of German war guilt. (*7 marks*)

**d)**   Study all the sources and use your own knowledge to explain how far you agree with the view that the Treaty of Versailles was not as harsh as it has later been argued. (*15 marks*)

Source questions often contain cartoons. Through exaggeration the cartoonist sets out to make a powerful comment on current events. Always ask yourself what is the message that the cartoon is communicating about the events or people portrayed. Here a furious German nationalist (Pan-German) is complaining about the terms of the peace, while conceding that any peace signed by a victorious Germany would have been much more severe. Is this a perceptive and fair comment on Germany's reaction to the peace?

Usually at least one source question asks you also to use 'your own knowledge' or 'any other evidence known to you'. Questions like this are really essays linked to specific sources. You must therefore take care to evaluate the given sources and draw on your own historical knowledge to add to them. Remember that you must reach a judgement. Usually your sources will be contradictory, or one-sided, allowing you to reach only a qualified answer. In 3d), for example, with the exception of Source D most of the sources emphasise Germany's past ambitions and the need to punish it for causing the war. To give a more balanced picture you need to point to some of the most punitive (punishing) clauses of the treaty such as the separation of Danzig and large areas of eastern Germany from the Reich, and consider whether these were unnecessarily harsh. You could also mention that the Germans themselves had overthrown the Kaiser and created a new democratic and apparently peace-loving democratic republic. What other information would you need to draw on from Chapter 2?

# 3 The Struggle to Enforce the Treaties, 1920–4

## POINTS TO CONSIDER

This chapter will examine Allied attempts to implement the peace treaties. First of all the consequences of the Russo-Polish war are examined. Then Anglo-French efforts to enforce the Treaty of Versailles, and above all to extract reparation payments from Germany, which culminated in the occupation of the Ruhr, are looked at. Finally the reasons why the Treaty of Sèvres failed are analysed. As you read through this chapter, your aim should be to understand why Britain and France increasingly disagreed on how to enforce the peace treaties.

## KEY DATES

| | | |
|---|---|---|
| **1920** | March | Allenstein-Marienwerder plebiscite |
| | March–October | Russo-Polish War |
| | August | Battle of Warsaw |
| **1921** | March | Plebiscite in Upper Silesia |
| | April | Reparation Commission fixed German debt at 132 milliard gold marks |
| | May | Fighting breaks out in Upper Silesia |
| **1922** | April | Genoa conference and Treaty of Rapallo signed between Germany and Soviet Russia |
| | 3 Sept–1 October | Chanak Incident |
| **1923** | 11 January | French and Belgian troops occupy the Ruhr |
| | July | Treaty of Sèvres finally revised at Lausanne Conference |
| **1924** | April | Dawes Commission published its recommendations |

## 1 The Organisation for Carrying out the Treaties

> **KEY ISSUE** What was the machinery for carrying out the peace treaties?

Once the peace treaties had been ratified, the wartime Allies had to devise means for ensuring that they were actually carried out. As the American Senate rejected the treaties, the main responsibility for carrying them out fell on Britain and France, which were given some limited assistance by Belgium, Italy and Japan. The *Entente* powers were faced with formidable problems:

- They had to organise plebiscites to decide the future of the German border territories in Schleswig, Allenstein, Marienwerder and

Upper Silesia, as well as in Sopron on the Austrian–Hungarian border;
- they also had to ensure that that the process of German disarmament was carried out according to the demands of the Treaty;
- and to establish the exact amount Germany owed in reparations.

After the Treaty of Versailles had been signed, the victorious powers set up a series of inter-Allied commissions to organise the plebiscites, monitor German disarmament and examine Germany's financial position with a view to its payment of reparations. These reported to the Conference (or committee) of Ambassadors in Paris, which represented the Allied powers, but the real decisions were taken by the Allied prime ministers, who between January 1920 and January 1924 met 24 times to review progress made in carrying out the peace. The League of Nations was ultimately responsible for the administration of the Saar and Danzig (see page 80), but initially the key decisions on these areas were taken by the Conference of Ambassadors and the Allied prime ministers.

## AMERICA AND THE PEACE TREATIES

President Wilson attempted to win popular backing at home for the Treaties, but on 26 September 1919 he suffered a massive stroke, which left him partly paralysed. Subsequently he failed to obtain the necessary two-thirds majority in the Senate to ratify the Treaties. The USA, did, however, later sign separate treaties with the ex-enemy states, and American troops stayed in the Rhineland until early 1923.

## 2 The Russian Problem

> **KEY ISSUE** Why did implementation of the peace treaties in Eastern Europe depend on the outcome of the Russian civil war and the Russo-Polish war?

The success of the peace treaties depended directly in eastern Europe, and also to a great extent in the Near East, on Russian acceptance of the decisions taken at Paris. The outcome of the Russian civil war was therefore of crucial importance. In the fluid situation of 1919–20 the western powers, Russia and the Germans pursued similarly ambivalent policies:

- The Bolsheviks tried to stir up revolution within central and western Europe, while at the same time establishing tentative diplomatic contacts with both the Germans and the Allies. They also tempted the Allied powers with the prospect of renewing trade

links and with talks on the possibility of repaying the former Tsarist regime's international debts;
- the Allies meanwhile maintained a naval blockade, but they too also wanted to keep open diplomatic contacts with Lenin as an insurance in case the Bolsheviks were victorious in the civil war. In April 1919, when the Whites were on the offensive and appeared to be winning the struggle, the Council of Four stepped up the dispatch of war material to them, although under pressure from Lloyd George and Wilson, who were anxious to avoid dangerously open ended military commitments, it also slowly began to evacuate the Allied troops sent to Russia in 1918 (see page 17). Only with the failure of the Whites in the winter of 1919–20 did the Allies raise the blockade and again give priority to the resumption of commercial and diplomatic contacts with Soviet Russia;
- the Germans were torn between impressing the Allies with their importance as a barrier against Bolshevism and so extracting concessions from them, and seeing the Bolsheviks as a potential ally against Britain and France, who would help them overthrow the Versailles settlement and destroy Poland.

As long as the Russian civil war lasted, neither the future of the Baltic states nor Poland's eastern frontiers could be fixed. Latvia and Estonia had been occupied by the Bolsheviks in the winter of 1918–19. An alliance of White Russians, Swedish and Finnish volunteers and a brigade of German Free Corps (see page 154) troops liberated them; but although the Allies ordered their withdrawal, they did not immediately recognise the independence of the Baltic states. In the event of a White victory in Russia, these states would almost certainly have been swallowed up by Russia, as the French ideally wanted a strong non-Bolshevik Russia to help keep Germany in check. The independence of the Baltic states was only assured when Bolshevik Russia recognised them in 1920.

The Poles exploited the chaos in Russia to seize as much territory as they could. In December 1919 they rejected the proposed eastern frontier based on recommendations put forward by Lord Curzon, the British Foreign Minister, and in early 1920 embarked on a full-scale invasion of the Ukraine. By August Bolshevik forces had pushed the Poles back to Warsaw. However, with the help of French military supplies and advisers the Poles rallied, and they managed to inflict a decisive defeat on the Red Army just outside Warsaw. Russian troops were pushed back, and in March 1921 Poland's eastern frontiers were at last fixed by the Treaty of Riga. Poland annexed a considerable area of Belorussia and the eastern Ukraine (see map, page 32), all of which lay well to the east of the proposed Curzon line. The way was now clear for the *Entente* powers to carry out the decisions of the Versailles Treaty without fear of intervention by Soviet Russia. The *Entente* was thus able to preserve its 'dominant voice in European stabilization'.[1]

# 3 Anglo-French Differences

> **KEY ISSUE**  Why did Britain and France disagree so bitterly on how to implement the Treaty of Versailles?

Both Britain and France had conflicting ideas of how best to ensure that Germany carried out the Treaty of Versailles. Essentially Britain, as the centre of a world-wide empire, wanted to see a balance of power in Europe that would prevent either French or German domination and leave it free to deal with the growing challenges to its power in India, Egypt and Ireland. It was convinced, too, that only a prosperous and peaceful Germany could pay reparations and play its part in Europe as one of the main engines of the European economy. For France, the German problem was an over-riding priority. French policy swung uneasily between occasionally exploring the possibilities of economic co-operation with Germany, and more usually of applying coercive measures designed permanently to weaken Germany and to force it to fulfil the Treaty. Britain increasingly opposed any further weakening of Germany, but was also concerned by Franco-German economic cooperation which might lead to the creation of an economic community capable of discriminating against British trade. Essentially neither country was strong enough to make its policies prevail. In the absence of help from America or of cooperation from a liberal and 'tamed' Germany, both remained ultimately dependent on the *Entente*.

# 4 Germany's Isolation

> **KEY ISSUE**  How could Germany achieve a revision of the treaty of Versailles?

The overriding aim of German foreign policy was to bring about, by any practical means, the revision of the Treaty of Versailles. In July 1919 Hermann Müller, the German foreign minister, laid down the guidelines for Germany's new foreign policy when he announced in the Reichstag that Germany had given up the use of military force and wished to reach a peaceful understanding with the *Entente* powers. Where it was at all possible, Germany would seek to carry out the Treaty, but it would nevertheless make every effort to achieve its peaceful revision.

In 1920 there were only two ways that Germany could hope to revise the Treaty. One was to exploit Anglo-French differences in the hope that these would weaken the Allies and lead to concessions to Germany. The other, favoured by the army, influential sections in the German Foreign Office, some industrialists and the German Communist Party, was to come to an understanding with Russia which would enable Germany to oppose Britain and France more effectively. However, this latter option was one which Berlin pursued with caution as it feared the spread of Communism. Yet when Soviet troops invaded Poland in the summer of 1920 (see page 48), it looked momentarily as if the whole structure of the Treaty, in eastern Europe at any rate, would crumble. German dockers refused to unload munitions for Poland in Danzig, and the German government declared its neutrality and refused to transport munitions across Germany to Poland, but their hopes were dashed by the battle of Warsaw.

In early 1920 Germany did achieve a small success by managing to play off France and Britain against each other over the issue of handing over German war criminals to be tried in Allied courts. By making secret contact with British officials on the Inter-Allied Military Control Commissions, which were just beginning to monitor the process of German disarmament, the Germans were able to persuade the British government that the depth of feeling in Germany against this demand was so intense that it would prevent the peace treaty from being carried out smoothly. The British government agreed, and persuaded the French that German war criminals should be tried only by German courts. This was, however, a one-off success for German diplomacy, and until the mid-1920s the Reich remained in Peter Krüger's words 'more an object of policy by the *Entente*'² than an independent power capable of pursuing its own foreign policy.

## 5 The Implementation of the Versailles Treaty in Eastern Europe

> **KEY ISSUES** Why were efforts to carry out the Treaty in Eastern Europe accompanied by bitter Anglo-French quarrels? Was it the British or French interpretation of the Treaty that eventually triumphed?

France had been forced to make considerable concessions over Germany's eastern frontiers with Poland (see page 31) and was determined to minimise, as far as possible, their actual impact on Poland. Thus in Danzig, Upper Silesia, Allenstein and Marienwerder bitter struggles were waged between French and British diplomats and soldiers in an effort to ensure that the wishes of their own governments would finally prevail.

### a) Danzig

Ultimately Danzig, according to the Treaty of Versailles, was to be placed under the protection of the League of Nations, but before this could happen the Poles and the Danzig Germans had to come to an agreement on the future commercial, economic and political relations between Poland and Danzig. The Poles insisted, with some justice, that the Treaty granted them control over the docks, railways, posts and telephones. If they could in fact achieve this, they would gain a stranglehold over what was supposed to be a free city. British officials both in Danzig and Paris consequently fought stubbornly to prevent it. In Paris the British Ambassador, Lord Derby, informed the Foreign Secretary in London that:

1  … if Poland is accorded the unrestricted rights in Danzig which she claims and which the French are apparently determined that she should have, Danzig becomes a dependency of Poland pure and simple and all idea of a Free City of Danzig or an amicable cooperation between the 5  two parties is excluded.... … The French are clearly determined by a rigid application of the letter of article 104 … to produce a situation in which the freedom of Danzig becomes nothing but a name. They evidently wish to revert, in fact, though not in theory, to the original recommendation of the Polish 10  Commission [the Allied officials working on the Polish frontiers in Paris in 1919] to include Danzig in Poland.

In the end the issue was referred to the Allied Prime Ministers at the Spa Conference in July 1920 and, despite French opposition, Britain was able to exploit Poland's dependence on Allied military aid to force it to accept the creation of a joint Polish–Danzig harbour board, which under a chairman appointed by the League of Nations would administer the docks. When the Free City was set up on 15 November, the British had won a significant diplomatic battle.

## b) The Schleswig, Marienwerder and Allenstein Plebiscites, 1920

These plebiscites were relatively simple operations, the outcome of which was predictable. Schleswig was divided into two zones. In the north the Danes won an overwhelming majority, while in the south the population voted to remain German. In Marienwerder and Allenstein, except for a few small pockets of territory, the overwhelming majority of the population also voted to stay German. In all three plebiscites there was considerable rivalry between British and French officials. The latter attempted in vain to champion the cause of the Poles and the Danes at the expense of the Germans.

## c) Upper Silesia, 1920–2

The task facing the Upper Silesian Plebiscite Commission[3] was as complex as any that confronted the *Entente* powers in Germany. The Commission in effect took over the government of Upper Silesia, a large Prussian province which contained a concentration of coal mines and iron and steel industries that was second only in size to the

Ruhr. It had a population of some 2,280,000 Germans and Poles, who were bitterly divided along ethnic lines. The Commission had not only to ensure law and order during what was to be a long and bitter plebiscite campaign, but also to guarantee the production of the coal, on which the economic life of so much of central Europe depended. Inevitably, then, Upper Silesia was the main focus in eastern Europe for Anglo-French rivalry. If at all possible, Britain was determined to prevent the further weakening of Germany by ensuring that Upper Silesia remained German, while France was determined that Poland should have it. Not only would it strengthen Poland, but it would make Germany even more dependent on the Ruhr mines in the West, which were vulnerable to French pressure from the Rhineland. The French, however, were in a strong position as they provided most of the army of occupation and filled the key posts on the Commission.

The plebiscite took place on 17 March 1921 in an atmosphere of relative calm, but it produced an ambiguous result which did not solve the Anglo-French disagreements over Poland. The British argued that its result justified keeping the key industrial region of the province German, while the French insisted that it should be awarded to Poland. Fearing that once again British wishes would prevail, an uprising broke out in May 1921. The Poles seized control of the industrial area, while the French refused to allow German troops to restore order and unofficially recognised the rebels' authority. Lloyd George, in a speech that reverberated through the capitals of Europe and caused a crisis in Anglo-French relations, pointedly argued that:

1 Either the Allies ought to insist upon the Treaty being respected, or they ought to allow the Germans to do it. Not merely to disarm Germany, but to say that such troops as she has got are not to be permitted to take part in restoring order in what, until the decision comes,
5 is their own province – that is not fair. Fair play is what England stands for, and I hope she will stand for it to the end.

The Germans, too, protested strongly, and *Freikorps* volunteers poured across the frontier to fight the Poles. The German government, with French troops occupying much of the Rhine (see page 31) did not dare openly support them, but it successfully pressed Britain to send a division of troops to restrain the Poles and the French. The view of the German government was expressed by Walther Rathenau on 22 May, a few days before he joined the cabinet as Minister for Reconstruction:

1 On August 4th 1914 the British Empire said 'Treaties must be kept.' And rightly, and these treaties must be held sacred between nations. Such a treaty was made between all civilised peoples of the world, and by twenty-eight nations. This treaty has lasted for two years. What has
5 happened to it? Where is the sanctity of the Treaty of Versailles? It has been nibbled at in the west and the east…We have had to endure

unspeakable things in Germany. Our country has been mutilated and
our resources are exhausted ... We are still a country with sixty million
inhabitants, and the world shall know that this nation is conscious of its
10 strength: not for war, but for work; and not only for work, but also for
the defence of our rights. We shall defend these rights by peaceful
means; but no one shall deprive us of them. And if, owing to unfortunate circumstances, irresponsible persons should dare to separate this
15 province [of Upper Silesia] from us, then it will be a sin whose consequences will lie far more heavily on the nations than Alsace-Lorraine. A
wound will have been made in Central Europe which will never close
and which can be only healed by justice.

Order was eventually restored by British and French troops in July,
but the deadlock between France and Britain over the future of
Upper Silesia was only broken by referring the whole question to the
League of Nations in August. The British hoped that the League
would rule in favour of a solution similar to the one it gave on the dispute between Finland and the Aaland islands (see pages 83–4), which
would have left German sovereignty over Upper Silesia intact, whilst
giving the Polish population self rule. Yet here Britain – and Germany
– were unlucky, as the League decided to hand over most of the
industrial areas to Poland. This time the French had won a significant
victory in their struggle to enforce their interpretation of the
Versailles Treaty on both Germany and Britain

# 6 Disarmament

> **KEY ISSUE** What differences were there between Britain and
> France over the question of disarming Germany?

The divisions between the British and French officials that had been
so evident on the plebiscite commissions were also present in the military Control Commissions that were monitoring German disarmament. By the end of 1922 the British were convinced that Germany
was effectively disarmed. With the German fleet destroyed Britain was
not threatened militarily by Germany, and consequently the Lloyd
George cabinet saw the disarmament question as less important than
the reparation issue and the revival of the German economy.

### THE GERMAN FLEET

The surface ships had been interned in Scapa Flow and the
submarines in Harwich. On 17 June 1919, to Britain's great
annoyance, the Germans managed to scupper their surface fleet.

To France, however, disarmament, as its prime minister, Aristide Briande, put it, was 'a question of life and death'.[4] Consequently the French took each German infringement of the disarmament clauses of the Treaty very seriously and were determined to keep up the pressure until Germany had totally disarmed. By the end of 1922 the British were anxious to see the Disarmament Commissions wound up, but the French, whose suspicions of German double-dealing were fuelled by the regular discovery of hidden weapons and secret mobilisation plans, were still bitterly opposed to a premature withdrawal of the Commissions.

# 7 Reparations

> **KEY ISSUE** What efforts were made to solve the reparation question by the end of 1922 and why did they all fail?

The German reparation problem came to dominate European diplomacy. Both the British and French hoped to solve the problem by fixing a global total as soon as possible on the assumption that once Germany knew the full sum of its debts it would be able to raise credit privately in America and begin payments. The French, however, contrary to the hard line they took over disarmament and the plebiscites, also explored the possibility of some kind of economic cooperation with Germany, which would effectively make Germany their junior partner. On 26 August 1920 the German Foreign Minister was informed through secret contacts that the French Minister of Finance

1   was disposed to talk unofficially with the German Government about the application of the financial clauses of the Treaty of Versailles ... The French government would abandon a part of its treaty rights, if in exchange for this very great concession, the German government
5   decides to give it satisfaction on other points. In brief, the treaty of Versailles appearing to many sensible people in France as 'not being able to stand on its own two feet', at least from a financial point of view, it would be desirable to go over it chapter by chapter in private conversation between representatives of the two governments and in a spirit
10  of mutual confidence. This would be but a first step toward a more far-reaching economic entente, which the French government has in mind, and which is in the interest of the two countries.

A first step towards the realisation of these ideas was the Seydoux Plan, which was produced by a French official, Jacques Seydoux. This would have allowed Germany to pay a large percentage of its reparation bill in industrial and plant deliveries, but it was rejected by both Britain and Germany at the Brussels Conference at the end of 1920. The Berlin Government was suspicious that still no exact figure had been given to the total reparations it would have to pay or deliver, and it also noted that France reserved the right to take action if Germany defaulted on the agreement. Besides, there was also considerable opposition from the German industrialists, who feared the French might exploit the treaty to dominate German heavy industry. Lloyd George, too, demanded that a definite figure be set and also opposed the Plan for fear that it would lead to a common economic front against Britain.

Nevertheless at the Paris Conference in January 1921 the Allies at last agreed on a provisional figure of 226,000 milliard gold marks to be paid over the period of 42 years. This caused an outcry in Germany and was immediately rejected by the German Government, which produced its own figures a month later. These amounted to a modest overall payment of 30 milliard gold marks, which was also conditional upon the retention of Upper Silesia. The offer was so obviously inadequate that the *Entente* occupied Düsseldorf, Duisburg and Ruhrort. As one German official conceded to a British officer on the IAMCC, Berlin had made a 'tremendous mistake in allowing France the opportunity of putting herself in the right'.[5] As a final gamble before the Reparation Commission came up with fresh figures on 1 May, the Germans appealed to America and produced a payments plan, which, had it been produced earlier, might have been acceptable; but the Americans at this stage still refused to be drawn into the reparation conflict. At the end of April 1921 the Reparation Commission at last fixed a global total for reparations of 132 milliard gold marks, which was considerably less than the amount provisionally fixed in Paris in January, although it was still greeted with an explosion of rage in Germany. The amount was accepted by the Allied leaders, who on 5 May dispatched an ultimatum to Berlin giving the Germans only a week to accept the new payment schedule, after which the Ruhr would be occupied. The response of the Germans to the Allied reparation demands had temporarily united Britain and France, although events in Upper Silesia in the summer of 1921 were soon to divide them (see above).

To carry out the London ultimatum a new government was formed by Joseph Wirth on 10 May. Assisted by Walther Rathenau, his Minister for Reconstruction, he was determined to pursue a policy of negotiation rather than confrontation. Rathenau pursued initiatives in both Paris and London which perhaps, given time, could have led to a solution to the reparation crisis. He attempted to revive a version of the Seydoux Plan when he signed the Wiesbaden Accords with Loucheur on 6 October, which would have increased the amount of reparations delivered in kind and envisaged 'direct Franco-German cooperation as the core of western European reconstruction'.[6] Yet by the autumn of 1921 this policy was running into considerable difficulties. On 31 August the first installment of reparations had been paid punctually, but, as this government, like its predecessors, still shied away from stabilising the currency, cutting expenditure and imposing new taxes, it was becoming ever clearer that Germany would not be able to pay the second installment punctually. Wirth and Rathenau, who became foreign minister in January 1922, were desperately seeking to gain time until the USA was ready to take part in a general reparation and inter-Allied debt settlement.

In December 1921 the German government dropped a bombshell by announcing that, as a consequence of escalating inflation, it could not raise sufficient hard currency to meet the next installment of reparation payments. This gave Lloyd George the opportunity to launch a major initiative. He, too, was convinced that Germany needed a temporary moratorium, or postponement of reparation payments, to put its economy in order, while in the longer term the key to the payment of reparations and a European economic revival lay in setting up a European alliance of industrial nations, including Germany, to rebuild Russia. This, Lloyd George hoped, would generate a trade boom from the profits of which Germany would be able to pay reparations without damaging the commerce of the other European nations. Briand agreed to discuss these plans at Genoa in the spring at a conference to which the Russians would also be invited, but he could only win backing from the French Chamber for Lloyd George's radical plans, if they were coupled with a British military guarantee of French security. Britain's refusal to commit itself to more than a short-term pact led to the resignation of Briand and his replacement by the hard liner Raymond Poincaré in January 1922.

The Genoa Conference was a disaster. Poincaré's veto on any attempt to negotiate a moratorium on reparations heightened the Germans' suspicions of his policies and led to a separate Russo-German economic agreement. The Germans feared particularly that he might use Article 116 of the Treaty of Versailles to encourage Russia to claim reparations (This article had originally been inserted to leave the door open to Russian claims in case the Whites won the civil war.) The Russians, on the other hand, were suspicious of Lloyd George's proposed economic alliance, made up as it was of capitalist states, and preferred to continue their policy of dividing the capitalist powers by negotiating individual agreements with them. Thus both Russia and Germany signed a bilateral agreement at Rapallo during the conference, in which each renounced any reparation or debt claims on the other. Germany also agreed to consult with Moscow before joining any international group set up to exploit the Russian economy. Rapallo effectively killed Lloyd George's plan. It is hard not to see Rapallo as a miscalculation by the Germans. While it did something to re-establish Germany's diplomatic freedom of manoeuvre, it also intensified both French and British suspicions of its motives.

In July 1922 another major confrontation between France and Germany seemed inevitable when the German government requested a 3-year moratorium. At the same time Britain announced that, as

America was demanding the repayment of British wartime debts, it must in turn insist on the repayment of an equivalent amount from its former allies. To the French, Britain's demand for these repayments contrasted painfully with the concessions Lloyd George was ready to offer the Germans. On 27 November the Poincaré cabinet decided finally that the occupation of the Ruhr was the only means of forcing Germany to pay reparations, and on 11 January French and Belgian troops moved into the Ruhr.

# 8 The Occupation of the Ruhr

**KEY ISSUE** Why did the Ruhr crisis mark a turning point in post war European history?

When French and Belgian troops marched into the Ruhr in January 1923, the *London Times* commented that 'something as far reaching in its effects as the declaration of war in 1914 or the conclusion of the armistice' had occurred.[7] The bitter Anglo-French debate over the interpretation of the Treaty of Versailles had reached a decisive stage. The British government, by not joining the French, signalled clearly that it believed that the restoration of the German economy was more important than the punctual payment of reparations, while the French persisted with their policy of implementing the Treaty of

A column of French troops on the way to Essen in the Ruhr, January 1923

Versailles by securing the Ruhr as a 'productive pledge' or guarantee that Germany would carry out the Treaty.

The Ruhr occupation presented Britain with a difficult dilemma: 'a breech with France would mean chaos in Europe',[8] which could even lead to a Franco-German war; on the other hand, concessions to France could lead to a French economic domination of the Continent or pro-longed chaos in the Ruhr. Britain consequently adopted a policy of 'benevolent passivity' towards France, which attempted, as the Cabinet minutes (records) put it, to minimise 'the adverse effects upon Anglo-French relations of French ... action and [to reduce] to a minimum the opportunities for friction upon the several inter-Allied bodies'.[9]

For 9 months the French occupation of the Ruhr was met by passive resistance and strikes which were financed by the German government. This increased the cost of the occupation, but it also triggered hyper-inflation in Germany. In September Germany was on the brink of collapse and the new Chancellor, Gustav Stresemann, had to call off passive resistance. The French then launched an all out offensive to detach the Ruhr and the Rhineland from Germany:

- they negotiated individual agreements with the big German firms to make special deliveries to France of coal and steel and to pay tax on any deliveries made to unoccupied Germany;
- parallel with these negotiations, plans were laid for the creation of a special bank for issuing a new Rhineland currency independent of the official German currency, the *Reichsmark*;
- similarly attempts were also made to set up an independent Rhine-Ruhr railway, which would control west German rail communications.
- The French also backed German Separatists in the Rhineland and Palatinate, who wished to break away from the Berlin government.

For a few weeks it looked as if France might, after all, succeed in creat-ing an independent Rhineland. To many Germans, calling off passive resistance was a humiliating surrender to France, and Stresemann himself compared it with the signing of the treaty of Versailles. Yet Germany was too weak to wage war and could only hope that Britain and America would in the end intervene to force a compromise on reparations. By January 1924 this policy was proved right. The French triumph was not as secure as it seemed. France, too, had exhausted itself and seriously weakened its currency, the franc, in the prolonged Ruhr crisis. Its attempts to back Rhineland Separatism and to create an independent Rhineland currency were unsuccessful. In the Palatinate the Separatist leaders were assassinated by German nationalist agents from unoccupied Germany or lynched by angry crowds. The Bank of England refused to back French plans for a Rhenish currency and instead invested £5 million in supporting the German government's ultimately successful efforts to stabilise the mark. Poincaré thus had little option but to cooperate with an Anglo-

American initiative for setting up a financial commission chaired by the American financier Charles G. Dawes, to examine the whole problem of how Germany could pay reparations.

The Ruhr crisis was a 'turning point in the history of post war Europe',[10] and marked the end of French attempts to carry out the Treaty of Versailles by force and the beginning of the gradual revision of the Treaty itself.

# 9  The Revision of the Treaty of Sèvres

> **KEY ISSUE**  How were the Turks able to achieve a revision of the Treaty of Sèvres? In what ways was the new Treaty of Lausanne more favourable to Turkey?

Although the Ruhr crisis eventually led to the Dawes Plan and some Allied concessions over the payment of reparations, the territorial clauses of the Treaty were untouched. In Turkey, however, the Allies were compelled under threat of war to revise the even harsher Treaty of Sèvres

Of all the treaties negotiated in 1919–20, Sèvres, signed on 10 August 1920, was the most obvious failure as it was never put into effect by the Turkish government. When the Allies imposed it, they took little account of the profound changes in Turkey brought about by the rise of Mustapha Kemal, the leader of the new nationalist movement. Kemal had set up a rebel government which controlled virtually the whole of the Turkish interior, and was determined not to accept the Treaty. Only if the Treaty had been imposed within the first few months of the Turkish defeat, before Kemal had built up support, might it have been successful; but the long delay until August 1920 ensured that growing Turkish resentment particularly at the Greek occupation of Smyrna, which the Allies had encouraged in May 1919, made its enforcement an impossibility.

To ensure the acceptance of the Treaty, an inter-Allied expedition occupied Constantinople in March 1920 and forced the Sultan to dismiss his Cabinet and declare Kemal a rebel. Inevitably this pushed Kemal into openly challenging the Treaty, thereby running the risk of a clash between the Kemalist and Allied forces. The French and Italians were unwilling to fight to enforce the Treaty but Lloyd George persuaded them to agree to allow Greek forces to advance from Smyrna and head off Kemal's threat to Constantinople. The initial success of the Greek army ensured that the Treaty was at last signed on 10 August, but only at the cost of escalating conflict with the Kemalist forces. Kemal was able to exploit Soviet Russia's suspicions that the western powers were aiming to destroy Bolshevism, to undermine the Treaty of Sèvres. A joint Russo-Turkish attack destroyed Armenia in

1920 (see the map on page 39), and the subsequent Treaty of March 1921, settling the Russo-Turkish frontier in the Caucasus, enabled Kemal to concentrate his forces against the Greeks without fear of Russian intervention from the north. By August 1922 he was poised to enter Constantinople and the Straits zone, which were still occupied by Allied troops. Both the Italians and French rapidly withdrew leaving the British isolated. Kemal, however, avoided direct confrontation with the British forces and negotiated an armistice, which gave him virtually all he wanted: the Greeks withdrew from eastern Thrace and Adrianople and the British recognised Turkish control over Constantinople and the Straits.

Although this incident, known as the Chanak crisis, contributed to Lloyd George's resignation, to the abdication of the Sultan of Turkey and to a decisive diplomatic defeat for Britain, paradoxically the subsequent international conference of Lausanne, which met to revise the Treaty of Sèvres, resulted in an agreement in July 1923 that has been described by Professor Anderson as 'a victory for the western and above all for the British point of view'.[11] Kemal, anxious not to be dependent on Russia agreed to the creation of small demilitarised zones on both sides of the Straits and the freedom of navigation through them for Britain, France, Italy and Japan. He also insisted on the abolition of foreign control over Turkish finances. This was a serious blow to the French hopes of re-establishing their pre-war influence over Turkish finances, and arguably they, apart from the Greeks, lost more than any other power as a consequence of the new Treaty of Lausanne.

The Chanak crisis in no way affected the fate of Turkey's former Arab provinces. In February 1919, in deference to Wilson and the Fourteen Points, Britain and France agreed that they could only exercise power over these territories in the name of the League of Nations. It took several more months of bitter argument before the British agreed to a French mandate in Syria and also French access to the oil wells in Mosul and Iraq. The frontiers between the British mandates of Palestine and Iraq and the French mandate of Syria were then finalised in December.

# 10 Assessment

> **KEY ISSUE** Why was Turkey a more successful revisionist power than Germany in this period?

By early 1924 the immediate postwar period was over. Both Britain and France had been dissatisfied with the Treaty of Versailles and each had attempted to revise it. Britain had managed to ensure that Danzig really remained a free city under the League, while France, despite the fact that 60% of the voters in the Upper Silesian plebiscite opted for Germany, was able to ensure that the vital industrial triangle went to Poland. Yet overall France's policy towards Germany was a disastrous failure. It failed neither to negotiate an 'economic *entente*' with Germany that would have slowly created an atmosphere of trust and economic cooperation between the two states, nor did it manage permanently to weaken Germany. France's final gamble in the Ruhr came close to success, but here too Britain's 'benevolent passivity' and its own financial weakness finally cheated it of success. Germany thus survived the dangerous postwar period and by the spring of 1924 was poised to make a come back as one of Europe's great powers.

Nevertheless, Germany remained shackled by the terms of the Treaty of Versailles. Unlike Turkey, it was unable to renegotiate the peace treaty. How was it that Turkey – and not the potentially much stronger Germany – was able to achieve such a revision? The Germans for a start lacked a dynamic leader like Kemal. Similarly they had no potential allies, once the Poles routed the Russians in August 1920. Kemal, on the other hand, was able to rely on Soviet support to regain Turkish Armenia and forcibly revise his country's eastern frontiers. He was confronted with a weak and divided Allied army of occupation. In Germany, on the other hand, there was a large French army, which was ready to fight if Berlin tried to revise the Treaty with force. In the end Germany survived and achieved some concessions over reparations not because of military resistance (although passive resistance in the Ruhr did play a role) but because France overreached itself in the Ruhr, and Britain and the USA were able to impose the Dawes Plan.

## References

1 W. McDougall, *France's Rhineland Diplomacy, 1914–24* (Princeton, Princeton University Press, 1978), p. 138.
2 P. Krüger, *Die Aussenpolitik der Republik von Weimar* (Darmstadt, Wissenschaftliche Buchgesellschaft, Darmstadt, 1985), p. 91.
3 For this section I have drawn on sections of my article on 'Implementing Versailles in the East, 1920–22' in *New Perspective*, vol. 5, no. 2, December 1999, pp. 6–10.
4 Quoted in D.G. Williamson, *The British in Germany* (Oxford, Berg Press, 1991), p. 184.
5 Ibid., p. 186.
6 C. Fink quoted in ibid., p. 151.
7 *The Times*, 6 January 1923.
8 R. Blake, *The Unknown Prime Minister* (London, Eyre & Spottiswoode, 1955), p. 485
9 Quoted in D.G. Williamson, 'Great Britain and the Ruhr Crisis, 1923–24' in *The British Journal of International Studies*, vol. 3, no.1, April 1977, p. 73.
10 L. Kochan, *The Struggle for Germany* (Edinburgh, Edinburgh University press, 1963), p. 29.
11 M.S. Anderson, *The Eastern Question* (London, Macmillan, 1966), p. 373.

**Summary Diagram**
Carrying out the Peace Treaties

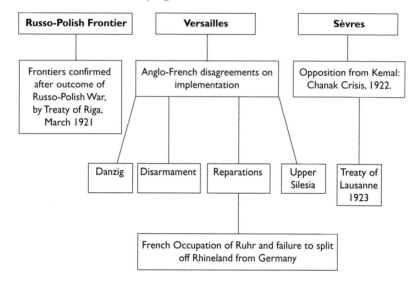

**Working on Chapter 3**

When making notes on this chapter, first of all identify the reasons why Britain and France each had a different approach to carrying out the Treaty of Versailles. You should stress that Versailles was a compromise peace and that both states attempted, even after they had signed the treaty, to interpret it according their own views. Once you have made this clear, you then need to look at what putting the peace treaty into practice involved: making the necessary arrangements for the transfer of Danzig to the League of Nations, carrying out the plebiscites, particularly in Upper Silesia, disarmament and then above all reparations. Consider especially why reparations were such a dominant issue in the period 1920–4, leading to the occupation of the Ruhr. Ask yourself why Germany could not oppose the *Entente* more effectively. Finally you need to ask why the occupation of the Ruhr was a turning point in postwar history. What were France's aims and why did it fail to achieve them despite its overwhelming military superiority? The German problem inevitably dominates immediate postwar history, but Turkey too faced a similar challenge of a harsh peace, Look carefully at how it was able to force the Allies, particularly Britain, to renegotiate Sèvres and also think how its position contrasted to Germany's.

## Answering structured and essay questions on Chapter 3

This chapter has involved a detailed analysis of the years 1920–3. It is important to have a good knowledge of this complex period because it helps explain Britain's attitude to Germany right up to early 1939, and why France had to give up its policy of enforcing the Treaty rigorously. Consider the following structured questions:

1 **a)** What tasks had the Allies to accomplish in Danzig? How easily were these achieved?
  **b)** What was the task of the Allied Plebiscite Commission in Upper Silesia and what problems did it encounter?
  **c)** Explain why Germany felt betrayed in Upper Silesia
2 **a)** How did France and Britain try to solve the reparation problem, 1920–3, and why was so little progress made?
  **b)** What did France intend to achieve when it occupied the Ruhr?
  **c)** Why did France fail to achieve these aims?

These questions are testing both your factual knowledge and understanding of the period. the first parts of 1a) and b) are quite straightforward, but the second parts of both questions, as well as 1c), require rather more analytical explanations. Both in 1a) and b) you need to explore Anglo-French differences over Germany as far as they affected Poland. In many ways it was these that caused most of the problems in these two areas. 1c) focuses more on Germany and the plebiscite result. You will need to explain why France felt it could override the result of the voting and how it managed to achieve its aims in Upper Silesia. In 2a) the first part of the question is essentially factual, and requires you to give a brief account of the whole reparation question from 1920 to 1923. Do not forget that the question of deliveries in kind, as considered in the Seydoux Plan and the Wiesbaden Agreement, comes into this! Similarly with 2b) you need to concern yourself with listing French intentions. The second half of 2a), as well as 2c), is more analytical. To answer why so little progress was made in the reparation question, you need to analyse the size of reparations demanded from Germany, Anglo-French differences and Germany's hope that the USA would eventually intervene and force a compromise over the whole reparation question. 2c) involves considering all the factors that in the end operated against a French success: the length of German passive resistance, Britain's 'benevolent passivity', the strength of German nationalism, etc.

The following are essay questions, which require a wider range of knowledge and more extensive answers:

1 'Revengeful and short sighted.' How accurate is this description of French policy towards Germany in the period 1920–3?
2 'Between 1920 and 1923 the future of Europe was decided by the outcome of the Anglo-French struggle over the interpretation of the Treaty of Versailles'. Discuss.

**3** Why was it the Treaty of Sèvres rather than the Treaty of Versailles that was revised by 1923?

Writing longer extended essays is one of the hardest tasks A-level students have to face. One of the keys to being able to write a good essay is not only to know the relevant information but also to have thought about the basic underlying questions in the period you are studying. Thus, as part of your revision, you should have planned out such basic questions as: 'What problems did the *Entente* meet with in attempting to implement the Treaty of Versailles?'; and 'What were the reasons for Anglo-French disagreement over implementing the Treaty, and what were the consequences of this?'. When you have thought these issues (and others) through, you ought not to be surprised by any essay question in the exam, as it is likely to be a 'dressed up' or elaborated versions of one of the key issues you have already planned. You will then be in a position to plan your essay much more quickly and to begin the main business of writing after perhaps 4 or 5 minutes' preparation.

As in most questions of this sort, the quotation in Question 1 is clearly one-sided. Your task is to assess its accuracy. On the one hand, France did attempt to exploit the Treaty in Danzig, Upper Silesia and the Ruhr to weaken Germany, but arguably it did this for security reasons, as the Anglo-American guarantee never in fact came into operation since the USA failed to ratify the Treaty. However, the Seydoux Plan and the negotiation of the Wiesbaden treaty indicate that Paris did keep open the option of an economic *entente* with Germany. Question 2 again asks you to consider a quotation, but it is less provocative. Clearly there is much to be said for the fact that the outcome of the Anglo-French struggle over the implementation of the Treaty did in fact shape Europe until 1936. The French victory in Upper Silesia decisively strengthened Poland, while France's failure in the Ruhr ensured that Germany could eventually re-emerge as a great European power and that a compromise would be found to defuse the reparation time bomb. This is the greater part of the answer, but always ask yourself whether there is anything that modifies or alters this approach. It would, for instance, be worth explaining that the outcome of the Polish–Soviet war in 1920 was crucial, as the Polish victory saved the Polish state and arguably the whole Treaty. The third question is a difficult comparative essay. If at all possible, it is best to approach such a question thematically, rather than spending the first section on Versailles and the second on Sèvres and then only making comparisons in the conclusion. Thus in one paragraph it would be a good idea to consider the question of Allied priorities. Clearly at Paris in 1919 the German treaty was a priority and Sèvres was left until 10 August 1920. This gave Kemal time to build up his forces and lead a successful rebellion against both the Sultan and the Treaty. A second paragraph could examine the geographical position of Germany and Turkey and note that the latter could rely on

Russian assistance, while Poland blocked Germany off from Russia. A third paragraph could look at the severity of the Treaties. Was Sèvres harsher than even Versailles? Did it arguably mean the virtual dismemberment of the Turkish state, while Versailles, harsh as it was, did leave most of Germany intact? Following on from there, a paragraph on the situation in both Germany and Turkey is needed. In Turkey the Sultan faced determined opposition from Kemal and the army. In Germany the Government had renounced force and hoped to modify Versailles through persuasion. There were, of course, many German Nationalists, like the members of the *Freikorps* who were only too willing to follow the example set by Kemal, but faced by Allied troops in the Rhineland and a large French presence in Upper Silesia, as well opposition from the German labour movement, they were not in a position to do much. Finally in Germany Britain did cooperate with France. Even during the Ruhr crisis British forces stayed in the Rhineland and were 'benevolently' passive. In the Chanak zone, both the Italians and the French withdrew leaving British troops to face the Turks alone. Here too one could mention that in eastern Germany the French relied on the Poles, while in Turkey the British relied on the Greeks in Smyrna, who were in a much weaker position than the Poles in Upper Silesia, who could easily obtain help from across the border to terrorise the German population.

## Source-based questions on Chapter 3

I   Revising the Treaties
Read the extracts on Danzig (Source A, page 51), Lloyd George's speech on Upper Silesia in the House of Commons on 13 May 1921 (Source B, page 52) and Walther Rathenau's speech on 22 May 1921 (Source C, pages 52–3), the secret French communication to the German Foreign Minister on August 1920 (Source D, page 54) and study the photograph on page 57 (Source E).
   a)   Study Source C
       What is meant by 'Our country has been mutilated' (line 7)? (*3 marks*)
   b)   Study Source D
       What is meant by 'economic *entente*' (line 11)? Explain why this was not achieved in the period 1920–3. (*7 marks*)
   c)   Using Sources A, B and C and your own knowledge, how far do you agree that the French were determined to strengthen Poland regardless of the Treaty of Versailles? (*10 marks*).
   d)   Using all the Sources and use your own knowledge, how far do you agree with the view that France was a far greater threat to the peace of Europe than Germany in the period 1920–3? (*20 marks*).

Questions a) and b) are testing your comprehension and factual knowledge. The most difficult questions here are c) and d), which are a mixture of a source-based and essay question. The key to answering them is to make linked use of your own knowledge and the sources in a confident and balanced way. Thus in Question c) you need to provide key background information (from Chapter 2) showing that the French felt cheated, as they had made many concessions on the understanding that Britain and America would sign a treaty guaranteeing French security. As this promise was not honoured, France was left alone and had to strengthen its position as best it could. In Danzig it was the British who were bending the letter of the Treaty, to carry out the compromise they had forced on France. Sources B and C contain some crucial evidence for answering the question, but to exploit it properly you must also use your background knowledge to stress that the French were supporting the Polish uprising to ensure that the industrial centre of Upper Silesia did not remain German despite the plebiscite result.

In Question d) the target is again making linked use of your own knowledge and the sources, but on a greater scale. You need to plan this as if you are writing an essay, but get the balance right between your own knowledge and the sources! A huge gap in the sources here, for instance, is the Ruhr occupation, which needs to be explored in your answer. How aggressive were France's intentions in the Ruhr?

When answering document questions, particularly on the twentieth century, you must be prepared to handle photographic evidence. Obviously you need to know the background of the events it records. Ask yourself what it shows and tells us about these events. Note, if possible, when and where the photo was taken. Has the photographer created a mood or selected a viewpoint to make us particularly aware of something? Are the people in the photo posing, or are they unaware of the camera? Is it propaganda? Remember that even if it is propaganda, it is still valuable to the historian because it shows what a government or political party wants us to believe.

# 4 The Politics of Reconciliation and Disarmament, 1924–30: The Locarno Era

## POINTS TO CONSIDER

This chapter covers the period after the failure of the Ruhr occupation when confrontation was slowly replaced with cooperation between Britain, France and Germany. It also looks at how the League of Nations grew in importance and became increasingly successful in solving local conflicts. The progress made towards disarmament is analysed, and so are the roles of the USA and USSR in the new politics of reconciliation. As you read this chapter, ask yourself both why the League was at last able to function more effectively and whether there really was a chance that Europe could now recover from the consequences of the First World War. Also consider whether America had in practice given up isolation.

## KEY DATES

| | | |
|---|---|---|
| **1921** | November | Washington Conference (till February 1922) |
| **1925** | 5–16 October | Locarno Conference |
| **1926** | January | Allies evacuated Cologne Zone |
| | 24 April | German–Soviet Treaty of Friendship |
| | September | Germany joined League of Nations |
| **1928** | 27 August | Kellogg–Briand Pact signed by 15 states |
| **1929** | August | Young Plan and Allied Evacuation of Rhineland approved |
| | 29 October | Wall Street Crash |

## 1 The Dawes Plan

**KEY ISSUES** What were the terms of the Dawes plan? How did it help stabilise Europe after the Ruhr Crisis?

The Dawes Plan played a crucial part in ending the bitter conflict over reparations, which had nearly escalated into open war during the Ruhr occupation. It was welcomed enthusiastically in April 1924 by the British Treasury as

the only constructive suggestion for escape from the present position, which if left must inevitably lead to war, open or concealed, between Germany and France.

However, like all international compromises, some powers had to compromise rather more than others. Although the Plan did not alter the overall reparation total, which had been fixed in 1921, it did recommend significant concessions:

- an 800 million gold mark loan, which was to be raised mainly in America, to assist the restoration of the German economy. This was a crucially important component of the plan because it opened the way for American investment in Germany;
- annual reparation payments were to start gradually and rise at the end of 5 years to their maximum level. These payments were to be guaranteed by the revenues of the German railways and of several key industries;
- a committee of foreign experts sitting in Berlin under the chairmanship of an American official was to ensure that the actual payments were transferred to the former Allies in such a way that the German economy was not damaged. The Plan was provisional and was to be renegotiated over the next 10 years.

There was much that the French disliked about the plan. For instance, it was not clear to them how the Germans could be compelled to pay if they again defaulted as they did in 1922. So they initially attempted to make their acceptance dependent on concessions from London and Washington on inter-allied debts and on the negotiation of a new security pact with Britain. The Americans threatened to withdraw from the Dawes Commission in the event of French non-acceptance, while Ramsay MacDonald, the new Labour British Prime Minister, vaguely promised to make a 'full exploration of the whole question of security'[1] once the Dawes Plan was implemented. With the defeat of Poincaré in the elections of June 1924 French willingness to cooperate markedly increased. Essentially, if the French were ever to receive any reparation payments and to avoid isolation, they had little option but to go along with the Dawes Plan.

The Germans also disliked the Plan as it placed their railways and some of their industry ultimately under international control and did nothing about scaling down their reparation debts. Stresemann, who, after the fall of his cabinet in November 1923, was now foreign minister, realised, however, that Germany had no alternative but to accept the Plan if the French were to be persuaded to evacuate the Ruhr sooner rather than later. Agreement to implement the Dawes Plan and to withdraw French and Belgian forces from the Ruhr within 12 months was achieved at the London Conference in August 1924. The new balance of power in Europe was clearly revealed when Britain and America devised a formula for effectively blocking France's ability to act alone against Germany in the event of another default in reparation payments. If Germany again refused to pay, it was agreed that

Britain as a member of the Reparation Commission would have the right to appeal to the International Court at the Hague and an American representative would immediately join the Reparation Commission. Joint Anglo-American pressure would then be more than enough to constrain France from reoccupying the Ruhr. Deprived of much of their influence on the Reparation Commission, the French had undoubtedly suffered a major diplomatic defeat at the London Conference.

# 2 The Locarno Agreements

> **KEY ISSUES** What were the terms of the Locarno Agreements; what did Britain, France and Germany gain from them; and why were they received with so much enthusiasm?

The Dawes Plan by bringing the Ruhr Crisis to an end had, together with the German measures to stabilise the mark, made Germany an attractive prospect for American investment. To a certain, extent one of the pre-conditions for a European economic recovery was now in place, but investment was to come from individuals and banks and was not guaranteed by the American government. Nor was it accompanied by offers of military security to the French. Thus should a new economic crisis blow up, American money could melt away and France could be left facing a strong and aggressive Germany. The French were therefore determined to plug this security gap. Initially the French looked to the League of Nations, where the Draft Treaty of Mutual Assistance or Geneva Protocol had been drawn up. This sought to provide world-wide security by obliging members of the League to come to the assistance of any state which was a victim of aggression and which was situated in the same continent as themselves. Yet by the time the British Labour Government was defeated in the election of October 1924 it was clear that no British Government with an empire spread all over the world could agree to become a world policeman on the scale required by the Geneva Protocol, and it was finally vetoed by the new Conservative Foreign Secretary, Austen Chamberlain, in March 1925.

The French had little option but to continue to insist, in as far as they still could, on the literal implementation of the Treaty of Versailles. They refused to agree to the evacuation of the Cologne Zone, which was due in January 1925 (see page 31), on the grounds that Germany had not yet carried out the military clauses of the Treaty 'either in the spirit or in the letter'.[2] The urgent need to reassure the French of Germany's peaceful intentions, and so secure the evacuation of Cologne, prompted Stresemann, on the unofficial advice of Lord D'Abernon, the British Ambassador in Berlin, to put forward a complex scheme for an international guarantee by the European great powers of the Rhineland and of the status quo in western Europe.

Chamberlain at first suspected the proposals of being an attempt to divide France and Britain, but he rapidly grasped that it was potentially a marvellous opportunity to square the circle by achieving both French security and the evacuation of Cologne without committing Britain to a military pact with France, which, as Chamberlain knew, the Cabinet would never tolerate. Briand was aware that only within the framework of an international agreement on the lines put forward by Stresemann could he in any way formally commit Britain to coming to the assistance of France.

In the ensuing negotiations Briand successfully persuaded Chamberlain and Stresemann to widen the international guarantee to cover the Belgo-German frontier. He also attempted to extend it to Germany's eastern frontiers, but this was rejected both by Stresemann and Chamberlain. However, Stresemann did offer arbitration agreements to Poland and Czechoslovakia, although he refused to recognise their frontiers with Germany as permanent. Chamberlain was quite specific that it was in British interests only to guarantee the status quo in western Europe. He told the House of Commons in November 1925:

> 1 A form of guarantee which is so general that we undertake exactly the
> same obligations in defence, shall I say of the Polish Corridor (for which
> no British Government ever will or ever can risk the bones of a British
> grenadier) as we extend to these international arrangements or con-
> 5 ditions on which, as our History shows, our national existence depends,
> is a guarantee so wide and general that it carries no conviction what-
> ever and gives no sense of security to those who are concerned in our
> action.

The negotiations were completed at the Locarno Conference, 5–16 October 1925. The Locarno Agreements consisted of:

- four arbitration treaties, signed by Germany with France, Belgium, Poland and Czechoslovakia;
- and of a Treaty of Mutual Guarantee, by which Belgium, Britain, France, Germany and Italy were bound to uphold the demilitarisation of the Rhineland and the existing frontiers between Belgium and Germany and France and Germany;
- the treaties were under-written by an Anglo-Italian guarantee to assist the victims of aggression;
- Italy had no direct interest in the Rhineland but was brought into the guarantee largely because France hoped it might act as a counter-weight to Britain's tendency to appease the Germans;
- Belgium, France and Germany also pledged themselves not to attack each other unless in self-defence. If a relatively minor incident on one of the frontiers covered by Locarno occurred, the

injured party (for example France) would first appeal to the Council of the League of Nations, and if the complaint was upheld, the guarantors would assist the injured state to secure compensation from the aggressor (for example Germany). In the event of a serious violation of the treaty the guarantors would act immediately, although they would still eventually refer the issue to the Council.

Throughout most of western Europe and America the Locarno Treaties were greeted with enormous enthusiasm. It appeared as if real peace had at last come. Had France now achieved the security it had for so long been seeking? Of all the great powers the French gained least from Locarno. It is true that France's eastern frontier was now secure, but under Locarno it could no longer threaten the Ruhr to bring pressure to bear on Berlin in the event of a war between its main eastern European ally, Poland, and Germany. The British had managed to give France the illusion of security, but the provision for referring all but major violations of the Locarno Agreements to the League before taking action ensured that the British government would in practice be able to determine, through its own representative on the Council, what action, if any, it should take. For Britain

After the signing of the Locarno Treaties in London. Briand stands in the middle of the front row; behind him, third from left, Stresemann; third row on left, Chamberlain (with monocle).

there were two main advantages to Locarno: it tied France down and prevented it from repeating the Ruhr occupation. Also, by improving relations between Germany and the Western Powers and by holding out the prospect of German membership of the League, it discouraged any close cooperation between Moscow and Berlin.

Locarno was deeply unpopular with the German nationalists, but for Stresemann it was the key to the gradual process of revising the

AFTER LOCARNO.

OLD MOTHER HUBBARD WENT TO THE CUPBOARD
TO GET HER POOR DOG A "SCRAP." . . .

After Locarno, *Punch* cartoon, 28 October, 1925.

Treaty. He wrote to the German ex-Crown Prince on 7 September 1925:

1   there are three great tasks that confront German foreign policy in the more immediate future. In the first place the solution of the Reparation question in a sense tolerable for Germany, and the assurance of peace, which is essential for the recovery of our strength. Secondly the pro-
5   tection of the Germans abroad, those 10 to 12 millions of our kindred who now live under a foreign yoke in foreign lands. The third great task is the readjustment of our Eastern frontiers: the recovery of Danzig, the Polish frontier, and a correction of the frontier of Upper Silesia.

By assuring Germany of peace in the west, and by not placing its eastern frontiers with Poland under international guarantee, Locarno left open the eventual possibility of revision of the German-Polish frontier. Stresemann's aims were therefore diametrically opposed to Briand's, but both desired peace and therein lay the real importance of Locarno. It was a symbol of a new age of reconciliation and cooperation. Locarno, as Ramsay MacDonald observed, brought about a 'miraculous change' of psychology on the Continent.[3]

# 3 The 'Locarno Spirit' and the Re-emergence of Germany as a Great Power

> **KEY ISSUE** To what extent did the Locarno treaties lead to a revision of the Treaty of Versailles?

The 'Locarno Spirit' was an elusive concept which was interpreted differently in London, Paris and Berlin. All three Powers agreed that it involved goodwill and concessions, yet the scope and timing of these concessions were a matter of constant and often bitter debate. Both Stresemann and Briand had to convince their countrymen that the Locarno policy was working. Briand had to show that he was not giving too much away, while Stresemann had to satisfy German public opinion that his policy of 'fulfilment' was resulting in real concessions from the ex-Allies. It can be argued that not only the survival of Stresemann's policy but of the German Republic itself depended on ever more ambitious diplomatic successes. What would happen once these were unobtainable?

## a) Stresemann's Initial Successes and Failures, 1925–7

The atmosphere of *détente* (easing of tensions) created by Locarno quickly led to the evacuation of the Cologne Zone in January 1926. As soon as the last troops departed, the Germans and many in the British Labour and Liberal parties claimed that the occupation of the remaining two Rhineland zones was increasingly an anachronism. In October 1926 Germany at last joined the League of Nations and received a permanent seat on the Council.

Stresemann exploited every opportunity both inside and outside the League to accelerate the revision of Versailles. One initiative in particular illustrates both the new informal approach to international politics during the Locarno era and the growing friendship between Stresemann and Briand. Over a gourmet meal in the village of Thoiry in France near the Swiss frontier, Stresemann outlined to Briand an ambitious scheme for bribing the French with a loan raised in America to evacuate the Rhineland and to return the Saar and its mines to Germany. Initially Briand showed considerable interest, but when it became clear that the Americans were not ready to subscribe to another loan and that by December, contrary to all expectations, the French Treasury had stabilised the franc, the deal was quietly shelved. Undaunted, Stresemann continued to wrest piecemeal concessions from the ex-Allies. In January 1927 the Allied Disarmament Commission was withdrawn from Germany, and in the following August Britain, France and Belgium withdrew a further 10,000 troops from their garrisons in the Rhineland.

## b) The Young Plan and the Evacuation of the Rhineland

In 1928 the German Government launched at Geneva a major initiative to persuade Britain and France to evacuate the Rhineland and, together with America, to agree to a revision of the Dawes Plan. The American bankers were ready to contemplate a revised reparations settlement as it was obvious that once the German Government had to pay the full annual instalments under the Dawes Plan, it would lack sufficient foreign exchange to meet the interest on the loans raised since 1924 in the USA. The French were ready to accept in principle a comprehensive international debt and reparations settlement and even the evacuation of the last two zones in the Rhineland, but Briand was determined to link this with setting up a new international body to ensure that the Rhineland remained demilitarised after evacuation.

The whole question of reparations was considered during the winter of 1928–9 by a committee of financial experts, which was chaired by the American banker, Owen Young. In June 1929 the Committee announced its recommendations:

- the overall reparation sum should be reduced from 132 milliard (gold) marks to 40 milliard (gold) marks and would be paid over the course of 59 years;
- the international controls over the German economy set up under the Dawes Plan would be dismantled;
- and the Reparation Commission would no longer be able to initiate sanctions.

The implementation of the Young Plan and the Rhineland question were discussed at the Hague Conference in August 1929. Initially Britain and France clashed bitterly over their share of reparations. The new Labour Chancellor of the Exchequer, Philip Snowden, was determined to demand compensation for the £200 million war debt payments, which the British Treasury had already made to the Americans, but eventually, after a dramatic midnight confrontation, he agreed to accept only 75% of his original demands. Over the Rhineland it was the French who dug in their heals in a last desperate attempt to extract concessions. It was only when Stresemann threatened not to sign the reparation agreement that Briand was forced to agree to its evacuation by 30 June. His plans for setting up a Commission of Verification and Conciliation to monitor demilitarisation had to be abandoned under joint Anglo-German pressure. The British feared that, far from conciliating, it would in fact deepen the differences between Germany and the ex-Allies.

The agreement to end the Rhineland occupation certainly helped make the Young Plan acceptable in Germany. In December the government had to face a referendum forced upon them by the Nazi and Nationalist parties declaring that its signature would be an act of high treason; but this was easily defeated and the Young Plan was officially implemented on 20 January 1930.

## c) Proposals for a European Customs Union and a Common Currency

With the evacuation of the Rhineland, Germany's restoration to the status of a great European power was virtually complete. Briand, like his successors in the 1950s, appears to have come to the conclusion that Germany could only be peacefully contained through some form of European federation. At the tenth Assembly of the League of Nations in 1929, he outlined an ambitious, but vague scheme:

1   I believe that there should be some kind of federal link between peoples who are grouped together geographically, like the peoples of Europe. These peoples should be able to come into contact at any time, to discuss their common interests, and to make a joint resol-
5   ution … Obviously the association will function most of all in the economic field: this is the most immediate necessity. I believe that in this field we can succeed. I am also sure, however, that from the political or social point of view, the federal link could be beneficial, without interfering with the sovereignty of any of the nations which might form part
10   of an association of this kind.

Stresemann reacted favourably and urged both a European customs union and a common currency. Briand was then entrusted by the 27 European members of the League with the task of formulating his plan more precisely; but when it was circulated to the chancelleries of

Europe in May 1930, the whole economic and political climate of Europe had dramatically changed. Stresemann had died and the political crisis in Germany caused by the onset of the Depression brought to power a government under Heinrich Brüning that was more interested in a customs union with Austria than in a European federation. The German Cabinet finally rejected the memorandum on 8 July 1930. A week later it was also rejected by Britain on the grounds that

> an exclusive and independent European union of the kind proposed might emphasise or create tendencies to inter-continental rivalries and hostilities which it is important in the genera interest to diminish and to avoid.

It is tempting to argue that this most dramatic sign of the Locarno spirit, which was killed off by the economic crisis that was eventually to bring Hitler to power, was one of the lost opportunities of history. On the other hand, it would be a mistake to view it through the eyes of early twenty-first century European federalists. Essentially Stresemann hoped that it would open the door to an accelerated revision of the Treaty of Versailles, while Briand calculated that it would have the opposite effect. Perhaps under favourable circumstances it could at least have provided a framework within which Franco-German differences could have been solved.

# 4 Russia and Eastern Europe

> **KEY ISSUES**  What role did Russia play in Europe in the Locarno era? To what extent did France consolidate its influence in Eastern Europe?

## a) Russia

The Soviet Government, which after the death of Lenin in January 1924 increasingly fell under the control of Stalin, viewed the progress made in stabilising western Europe through the Dawes Plan and the Locarno Agreements with both dismay and hostility, as it feared that this would strengthen the anti-Bolshevik forces in Europe and delay revolution in Germany. The Russians initially attempted to deflect Stresemann from his Locarno policy, first with the offer of a military alliance against Poland, and then, when that did not work, with the contradictory threat of joining with France to guarantee Poland's western frontiers. Stresemann, aware of Russia's attempts to stir up revolution in Germany in 1923, was not ready to abandon the Locarno policy, but he was anxious to keep open his links with Moscow and consolidate the Rapallo Agreement of 1922 (see page 56), if only as a possible insurance against Anglo-French pressure in the west. Thus the Russians were able first to negotiate a commercial treaty with Germany in October 1925. Then in April 1926, at a time when the Poles and the French were trying to delay Germany's membership of the League Council, they persuaded Stresemann to sign the Berlin Treaty. Essentially, this was a neutrality pact in which both powers agreed to remain neutral if either party was attacked by a third power.

Relations between Russia and Britain sharply deteriorated when the incoming Conservative Government refused in October 1924 to ratify the Anglo-Soviet General Treaty which had been negotiated by the outgoing Labour administration. In 1927, after ordering a raid on the offices of the official Soviet trading company, *Arcos*, in an attempt to discover evidence of espionage, the British Government severed all official relations with Russia. Only in 1929 with the return of Labour were ambassadors again exchanged. This outbreak of the first 'Anglo-Soviet cold war',[4] as the American historian Jacobson has called it, strengthened Stalin's determination to cut Russia off from the West. Increasingly the main thrust of Soviet foreign policy in the late 1920s was to exploit anti-western feeling in the Middle East, China and India.

## b) Poland and the Balkans

With the victory of the Bolsheviks in the Russian Civil War, the French began to build up a series of alliances in eastern Europe to take the place of their original prewar alliance with Tsarist Russia. In March 1921 they concluded an alliance with Poland which, because it was hated by Russia and Germany and was on bad terms with Czechoslovakia and Lithuania, was the most vulnerable of the east European states. Further French attempts to strengthen it met with little success. Paris failed to persuade Stresemann to agree to a permanent guarantee of Poland's frontiers or to ensure that Poland gained a permanent seat on the League Council. In 1925–6 it even looked as if the Polish state would suffer financial collapse, but by 1927 its financial position stabilised and for the time being the USSR and Germany had to tolerate its existence.

The French were less successful in organising the other new states created at Versailles into a defensive alliance against Germany. In August 1920 Czechoslovakia and Yugoslavia signed a pact which became known as the Little *Entente*, and were joined by Romania in 1921. However, it was primarily directed against Hungary and was designed to prevent the return of the Habsburgs and the revision of the Trianon Treaty. Only in 1924 did Paris succeed in concluding a treaty with Czechoslovakia but, again, it was not strictly an anti-German alignment. It would only come into operation in the event of a restoration of the royal families of Austria or Germany or of an Austrian *Anschluss* (union) with Germany. Despite attempts by Italy to challenge French influence in the Balkans, the French government was able to exploit the suspicions caused by the growth of Italian influence in Albania first to sign a treaty with Romania guaranteeing its frontiers (1926) and then a treaty of friendship with Yugoslavia (1927). By the end of the decade French influence was preponderant in the Balkans.

# 5 The League of Nations

> **KEY ISSUES** How did the League of Nations work, what were its responsibilities and how successful was it?

The League was a part of the international settlements negotiated in 1919–20. Inevitably the tensions and divisions inherent in these were also present in the League. The absence in 1920 of three great powers from the League reflected the reality of the international situation where both Germany and the USSR licked their wounds in defensive isolation, while the American Government, after having played such a key role in negotiating the new peace settlement, had been forced by Congress to disengage from most of its international responsibilities. The League's ultimate success or failure was dependent on the progress made by the great powers in stabilising Europe after the First World War. Not surprisingly the League's golden age coincided with the new stability created by the Locarno era.

## a) Its Constitution

In retrospect, it is possible to argue that the League's constitution provided too many loopholes for war, supported the status quo which favoured the great powers and, in the final analysis, lacked the machinery for collective action against an aggressor. Yet even if it had a theoretically perfect constitution, would its history have been any different? Perhaps the official British commentary on the Covenant was realistic when it pointed out:

1 If the nations of the future are in the main selfish, grasping and warlike, no instrument or machinery will restrain them. It is only possible to establish an organisation which may make peaceful cooperation easy and hence customary, and to trust in the influence of custom to mould 5 opinion.

The initial members of the League were the 32 Allied states which had signed the peace treaties and 12 neutral states. By 1926 all the ex-enemy states including Germany had joined, but Soviet Russia did not do so until 1934, and the USA never did. The League at first consisted of three main organs: the Assembly, the Council and the Secretariat. The Assembly was essentially a deliberative chamber where each state, regardless of its size, was allotted three representatives. It was a jealously guarded principle that even the smallest state had the right to be heard on international issues. The Council in 1920 had four permanent members: Britain, France, Italy and Japan. In 1926 this was increased by one when Germany joined. The smaller states were represented by a changing rota of four temporary members, later increased to seven, who were all selected by the Assembly. As the Council met more frequently than the Assembly and was dominated by the great powers, it gradually developed as an executive committee or 'cabinet' of the Assembly, and worked out the details and implementation of policies which the Assembly had endorsed in principle. Decisions in both bodies were normally taken by unanimous vote. The votes of states involved in a dispute under discussion by the League were discounted when the Assembly and Council voted on recommendations for its settlement. In this way they could be prevented from vetoing an otherwise unanimous decision.

The routine administrative work of the League was carried out by the Permanent Secretariat which was staffed by a relatively small international civil service. In 1921 a fourth organ was added to the League when the Permanent Court of International Justice was set up at The Hague (in the Netherlands) with the task of both advising the Council on legal matters and of judging cases submitted to it by individual states. The League was also committed to setting up a permanent commission to advise the Council on 'all matters relating to the observance of the mandates' and to undertake a whole series of social and economic obligations ranging from maintaining 'fair and humane conditions of labour for men and children' to the international 'prevention and control of disease' (articles 22 & 23).

The heart of the Covenant, articles 8–17, was primarily concerned with the overriding question of the prevention of war. The League's long-term strategy for creating a peaceful world was summed up in the first section of Article 8:

The Members of the League recognise that the maintenance of peace requires the reduction of national armaments to the lowest point consistent with national safety, and the enforcement by common action of international obligations.

The process for solving disputes between sovereign powers was defined in articles 12–17. Initially (Article 12) disputes were to be submitted to some form of arbitration or enquiry by the League. While this was happening there was to be a cooling-off period of 3 months. By Article 13 members were committed to carrying out the judgements of the Permanent Court of International Justice or the recommendations of the Council. Even if a dispute was not submitted to arbitration, the Council was empowered by Article 15 to set up an enquiry into its origins. The assumption in these Articles was that states would be only too willing to eliminate war by making use of the

League's arbitration machinery. If, however, a state ignored the League's recommendations, Article 16 made it clear that

I I ... it shall ... be deemed to have committed an act of war against all other Members of the League, which hereby undertake immediately to subject it to the severance of all trade or financial relations ...

II It shall be the duty of the Council in such case to recommend to the
5 several Governments concerned what effective military, naval or air force the Members of the League shall severally contribute to the armed forces to be used to protect the Covenants of the League.

In Article 17 the League's powers were significantly extended by its right to intervene in disputes between non-members of the League, while in Article 11 member states were encouraged to refer to the Assembly or Council any international problem which might threaten the peace.

In theory the League seemed to have formidable powers, but it was not a world government in the making, with powers to coerce independent nations. Its existence was based, as Article 10 made clear, on the recognition of the political and territorial independence of all member states. Article 15, for instance, recognised that if a dispute arose from an internal issue, the League had no right to intervene. There were, too, several gaps in the League Covenant which allowed a potential aggressor to wage war with impunity. War had to be officially declared before the League could act effectively. It had, for instance, no formula for dealing with acts of guerrilla warfare, which the instigating state could disown. Even in the event of a formal declaration of war, if the international Court or the Council could not agree on a verdict, then League members were free to continue with their war.

## b) The League Struggles to Find a Role

In January 1920 the governments of the great powers viewed the League with either cynicism or open hostility. The French doubted its ability to outlaw war, while the Germans saw it as a means for enforcing the hated Versailles Treaty. For a short time after the Republican victory in November 1920 the American government was openly hostile to the League and its officials were instructed to avoid any cooperation with the organisation.

Under the Treaty the League was responsible for the administration of the Saarland and Danzig. This inevitably involved the danger of it becoming too closely associated with the policy of the Allies. Indeed, in the Saarland, it made the mistake of appointing a French chairman to the governing commission which then administered the territory in the interests of France. In Danzig the role of the League was also regarded with great suspicion by the Germans. By Article 101 of the Treaty the League was to appoint a high commissioner who was to act as a mediator between the Poles and the Danzigers. Inevitably he came to be seen as the agent of the Allies enforcing the Treaty of Versailles. The League was also the guarantor of the agreements, signed by the Allies and the successor states created in 1919, which were aimed at ensuring that the various racial minorities left isolated behind the new frontiers enjoyed full civil rights.

Given the hostility or indifference which initially surrounded the League, it is understandable that initially the Council decided to concentrate on the less controversial areas where progress could be made. Thus committees were set up to monitor the administration of the mandates and implement the economic and social objectives contained in Article 23. In the long term it was with this work that the League was to be most successful.

## c) The Mandates

Article 22 of the Covenant marked a potentially revolutionary new concept in international affairs:

1   To those colonies and territories, which as a consequence of the late
    war have ceased to be under the sovereignty of the States which have
    formerly governed them, and which are inhabited by peoples not yet
    able to stand by themselves under the strenuous conditions of the
5   modern world, there should be applied the principle that the well-being
    and development of such peoples should form a sacred trust of civilis-
    ation, and that securities for the performance of this trust should be
    embodied in this covenant.

When the Allies distributed the former German and Turkish territories amongst themselves, these were divided into three groups according to how developed these were. The most advanced were in the Middle East, while the most backward were the ex-German islands in the Pacific. The League's greatest task was to avoid becoming a facade for colonialism in a new form. Thus it challenged the argument of the South African Prime Minister that their mandate over South West Africa was 'annexation in all but name'.[5] The mandate powers were required to send in annual reports on their territories to the League's Permanent Mandates Commission, which rapidly gained a formidable reputation for its expertise and authority. Whenever there were riots or disturbances in the mandates, the Commission set up a committee of enquiry which asked searching and sometimes embarrassing questions. For instance, in Palestine the British were criticised for being too pro-Arab in 1930.

The League's attitude towards the mandates was by modern standards paternalistic and condescending, but nevertheless, as Northedge has argued, 'it helped transform the entire climate of colonialism',[6] since the imperialist powers were forced by moral pressure to consider the interests of the native populations and to begin to contemplate the possibility of their eventual independence.

## d) The League's Social and Economic Work

Many League officials were convinced that the gradual forging of international technical medical and social links would do much to create a more peaceful world. According to a contemporary expert on the League, Alfred Zimmern, it was believed that

1  Little by little … the morass of high politics would dry up along its edges, as one issue after another was drained off to Geneva. Thus eventually there would be a worldwide cooperative system held together by a network of contacts between government departments
5  professional organisations and individual experts.

The League was excluded from dealing with the key financial issues of reparations and war debts, but nevertheless in 1922 its Financial Committee was entrusted by the Allied leaders with the task of rebuilding first Austria's and then Hungary's economy. Its Economic Committee had the far greater task of attempting to persuade the powers to abolish their tariffs and create a world-wide free trade zone. It organised two world economic conferences, held in 1927 and 1933, which both Soviet Russia and the USA attended. But not surprisingly, given the strongly protectionist economic climate of the times, it failed to make any progress towards free trade. Its social policy was more successful.

One of the greatest successes of the League was the International Labour Organisation (ILO). This had originally been created as an independent organisation by the Treaty of Versailles, but it was financed by the League. In some ways it was a league in miniature. It had its own permanent labour office at Geneva, staffed by a thousand officials. Its work was discussed annually by a conference of labour delegates. Right up to 1939 the ILO turned out an impressive stream of reports, recommendations and statistics which provided important information for a wide range of industries all over the world. The League's Health Organisation provided an invaluable forum for drawing up common policies on such matters as the treatment of diseases, the design of hospitals and health education. The League also set up committees to advise on the limiting of production of opium and other addictive drugs, on the outlawing of the sale of women and children for prostitution and on the effective abolition of slavery.

## e) The League as Peace-maker and Arbitrator, 1920–5

Until 1926, when the foreign ministers of Britain, France and Germany began to attend the meetings of the Council and turn it into a body which regularly discussed the main problems of the day, the

League of Nation's role in the many postwar crises was subordinated to the Allied leaders and the Conference of Ambassadors, which had been set up to supervise the carrying out of the Treaty of Versailles. For the most part it therefore dealt with minor crises only.

In 1920 the inability of the League to act effectively without the backing of the great powers was clearly demonstrated. In May Persia appealed to the League for assistance when Soviet forces crossed its northern frontier. Fortunately for the League, as it was unsupported in this issue by any great power, the appeal could be dismissed on the grounds that negotiations were already in fact taking place between Moscow and Teheran. The League also failed to protect Armenia from a joint Russo-Turkish attack, even though the Supreme Council had played with the idea of making it a mandate, as again none of the great powers was ready to protect it with force. One of the French delegates caustically observed in the Assembly that he and his colleagues were

> in the ridiculous position of an Assembly which considers what steps should be taken, though it is perfectly aware that it is impossible for them to be carried out.

In October 1920, in response to appeals from the Polish Foreign Minister, the League negotiated an armistice between Poland and Lithuania, whose quarrel over border territories was rapidly escalating into war. The ceasefire did not, however, hold, as shortly afterwards General Zeligowski with a Polish force, which the Warsaw government diplomatically pretended was acting on its own initiative, occupied the city of Vilna and set up the new puppet Government of Central Lithuania under his protection. The League first called for a plebiscite and then, when this was rejected, attempted in vain to negotiate a compromise settlement. In March 1922 Poland finally annexed Vilna province. A year later, after it was obvious that the League could not impose a solution without the support of the great powers, the Conference of Ambassadors took the matter into its own hands and recognised Polish sovereignty over Vilna. Britain, France and Italy, by failing to use the machinery of the League to stop Polish aggression, had again effectively marginalised it.

In less stubborn disputes, however, where the states involved were willing to accept a verdict, the League did have an important role to play as mediator. The League enjoyed a rare success in the dispute between Finland and Sweden over the Aaland Islands. These had belonged to the Grand Duchy of Finland when it had been part of the Russian Empire. Once it had broken away from Russia in 1917, the islanders, who were ethnically Swedish, appealed to Stockholm to take over the islands. When Sweden began to threaten force, the British referred the matter to the League. In 1921 the League supported the status quo by leaving the islands under Finnish sovereignty, but insisted on itself ensuring the civil rights of the Swedish population there. Neither government liked the verdict, but both accepted it and, what is more important, made it work.

In the second half of 1921 the League did serve as a useful means of focusing the attention of the great powers on the plight of Albania when it urgently appealed for help against Greek and Yugoslav aggression. As the Conference Ambassadors had not yet finally fixed its frontiers, the Greeks and Yugoslavs were exploiting the ambiguous situation to occupy as much Albanian territory as they could. The Council responded by despatching a commission of enquiry, but it took a telegram from Lloyd George both to galvanise the Conference of Ambassadors into finalising the frontiers and to push the League Council into threatening economic sanctions against Yugoslavia if it did not recognise them. When this was successful, the League was then entrusted with supervising the Yugoslav withdrawal. Thus in this crisis the League had played a useful but again secondary role to the Allied powers. The fact that the Conference of Ambassadors then made Italy the protector of Albania's independence indicates where the real power lay.

In August 1921 the League played a key role in solving the bitter Anglo-French dispute over the Upper Silesia plebiscite, which was referred to the League Council (pages 51–3). It again proved useful in the protracted dispute over Memel. When the Lithuanians objected to the decision by the Conference of Ambassadors to internationalise the port of Memel, and seized the port themselves in 1923, the League was the obvious body to sort out the problem. Its decision for Lithuania was accepted by the Allies.

Attempts by Britain and Sweden to refer the question of the Ruhr occupation of 1923 (see pages 57–9) to the League were blocked by the French, who had no intention of allowing the League to mediate between themselves and the Germans. In the Corfu incident of August–September 1923 the League's efforts to intervene were yet again blocked by a great power. The crisis was triggered by the assassination in Greek territory near the Albanian frontier of three Italians, who were part of an Allied team tracing the Albanian frontiers for the Conference of Ambassadors. Mussolini, the Italian Fascist Prime Minister, who had come to power the preceding October, immediately seized the chance to issue a deliberately unacceptable ultimatum to Athens. When the Greeks rejected three of its demands, Italian troops occupied Corfu. The Greeks wanted to refer the incident to the League, while the Italians insisted that the Conference of Ambassadors should deal with it. The Conference, while initially accepting some assistance from the League, nevertheless ultimately settled the case itself and insisted that Greece should pay 50 million lire in compensation to Italy. Once this was agreed, Italian forces were withdrawn from Corfu. The Corfu incident, like the Ruhr crisis, underlined the continuing ability of the great powers to ignore the League and to take unilateral action when it pleased them.

In 1924 the League was confronted with another crisis involving a greater power and a lesser power. On this occasion it was able to mediate successfully. It provided a face-saving means of retreat for Turkey in its dispute with Britain over the future of Mosul, which according to the Treaty of Lausanne (see page 60) was to be decided by direct Anglo-Turkish negotiations. When these talks broke down and the British issued in October 1924 an ultimatum to Turkey to withdraw its forces within 48 hours, the League intervened and recommended a temporary demarcation line, behind which the Turkish forces withdrew. It then sent a commission of enquiry to consult the local Kurdish population, which, as total independence was not an option, preferred British to Turkish rule. The League's recommendation that Mosul should become a mandate of Iraq for 25 years was then accepted. As Iraq was a British mandate, this effectively put it under British control.

In October 1925, the League's handling of the Greece–Bulgarian conflict, like its solution to the Aaland Island dispute, was to be a rare example of a complete success. When the Bulgarians appealed to the Council, its request for a ceasefire was heeded immediately by both sides. So too was the verdict of its commission of enquiry, which found in favour of Bulgaria. It was an impressive example of what the League could do, and in the autumn of 1925 this success, together with the new 'Locarno spirit', seemed to auger well for the future. Briand stressed at the meeting of the Council in October 1925:

1  It had been shown that the criticisms which had been brought against the League of Nations to the effect that its machinery was cumbersome and that it found it difficult to take action in circumstances which required an urgent solution were unjustified. It has been proved that a
5  nation which appealed to the League when it felt that its existence was threatened, could be sure that the Council would be at its post ready to undertake its work of conciliation.

The League was not put to the test again until the Manchurian crisis of 1931. Unfortunately Briand's optimism was to be shown to be premature (see page 97–9).

# 6 The League, America and Disarmament

> **KEY ISSUES** What role did the USA play in the disarmament question, 1921–33? Why was the League able to achieve so little on this issue?

One of the major tasks of the League was to work out an acceptable world disarmament programme. Disarmament, however, could not be divorced from the question of security, for if a state did not feel secure, it would hardly disarm. Thus on the initiative of the French the Assembly adopted a resolution in September 1922 which specifically linked these two aims. In 1924 the League did attempt to draft an ambitious collective security agreement, the Geneva Protocol (see page 69), but it was rejected by Britain, who feared that it would commit it to policing the world. Britain preferred more precise regional agreements, or as Austen Chamberlain put it: 'special arrangements to meet special needs'.[7]

Chamberlain was primarily thinking of Locarno when he made this remark, but with America outside the League the twin problems of growing Anglo-American naval rivalry and deteriorating American–Japanese relations in the Pacific had also been tackled on a largely regional basis. In 1919 America had been alarmed by the rise of Japanese power in the Pacific. Japan, already possessing the third largest navy in the world, had begun a major naval construction programme. The Americans responded by forming a Pacific fleet and embarking on their own formidable building programme, which, when completed, would make the American navy the largest in the world. In turn this pushed Britain in early 1921 into announcing its own naval programme, but privately it was intimated to Washington that a negotiated settlement was desired as Britain could not afford a naval race. President Harding was anxious both to reduce armaments and to economise, but he would only negotiate with Britain if it agreed not to prolong the 20-year-old Anglo-Japanese alliance which, theoretically at least, could have involved Britain as Japan's ally in a war against America. As the treaty was due for renewal in July 1921 the British and Japanese agreed under pressure from Washington to replace it by a new four-power treaty, which committed Britain, France, Japan and the USA to respect each other's possessions in the Pacific and to refer any dispute arising out of this agreement to a conference of the four signatory Powers.

With the Anglo-Japanese Treaty out of the way, the first Washington Treaty was signed in February 1922 for a duration of 14 years. It halted the building of capital ships for 10 years, provided for the scrapping of certain battleships and battle cruisers, and, for those capital ships which were spared the breaker's yard, established a ratio of 3 for Japan and 1.67 each for Italy and France to every 5 for Britain and the USA. In 1929 Britain, Japan and the USA in the London Naval Treaty agreed to extend the main principle of this agreement to smaller fighting ships.

From 1922 onwards the USAs' attitude towards the League began to alter. It saw the value of participating in some of the League's committees on social, economic and health matters, and President Harding even considered American membership of the Permanent Court of International Justice in 1923, but the Senate again vetoed it. When the League set up a Preparatory Commission in 1926 to prepare for a world disarmament conference, both the USA and Soviet

Russia participated. Peace movements, especially the American Committee for the Outlawry of War and the Carnegie Endowment for International Peace, exerted considerable pressure on the American Government to play a greater role. In March 1927, Professor Shotwell, a director of the Carnegie Endowment, on a visit to Paris persuaded Briand to sign a message and sent it over the head of the President to the American people, proposing a Franco-American pact that would outlaw war. Briand was, of course, delighted at any chance to involve America, even if indirectly, in the French postwar alliance system. To avoid just such a linkage Kellogg, the American Secretary of State, replied cautiously in December suggesting a general pact between as many states as possible, rejecting war 'as an instrument of national policy'. Briand had no alternative but to accept it, if he wished to ensure American cooperation. Thus on 27 August 1928 the Kellogg–Briand Peace Pact was signed by 15 states, and by 1933 a further 50 had joined it. It consisted of three articles only:

1.  1. The high contracting parties solemnly declare in the names of their respective peoples that they condemn recourse to war for the solution of international controversies, and renounce it as an instrument of national policy in their relations with one another.
5.  2. The high contracting parties agree that the settlement or solution of all disputes or conflicts of whatever nature or of whatever origin they may be, which may arise among them, shall never be sought except by pacific means.
   3. This treaty ... shall remain open ... for adherence by all the other
10.    Powers of the world.

Optimists saw the Pact as supplementing the Covenant. It outlawed war, while the League had the necessary machinery for setting up commissions of inquiry and implementing cooling off periods in the event of a dispute. Pessimists, however, pointed to the fact that it was just a general declaration of intention, which did not commit its members. Perhaps, in reality, all that could be said for it was that it would give the American Government a moral basis on which it could intervene in world affairs, should it desire to do so. In 1946 the pact provided the legal basis for charging the Nazi leaders with the crime of waging aggressive war at the Nuremberg trials.

In 1930 the Preparatory Commission, after protracted discussions on different models of disarmament, produced its final draft for an international convention. The League Council called the long-awaited World Disarmament Conference in February 1932 at Geneva. It could not have been convened at a more unfortunate time: the Manchurian crisis was escalating into full-scale war between China and Japan (see pages 97–9), the rise of nationalism in Germany was making France and Poland less likely to compromise over German demands for equality in armaments, while the impact of the Depression on the USA was reviving the isolationist tendencies of the early 1920s. Long before the Germans withdrew in November 1933 (page 101) it was clear that the Conference would fail.

# 7 Assessment

**KEY ISSUE**  To what extent did the Locarno Agreements mark the beginning of a new era of conciliation?

The acceptance of the Dawes Plan and the signature of the Locarno Agreements together marked a fresh start after the bitterness of the immediate postwar years. For the next 4 years the pace of international cooperation quickened and the League of Nations, despite a hesitant start, grew in authority and influence. After Germany joined the League in 1926 a new framework for great power cooperation evolved. The foreign ministers of Britain, France and Germany (Austen Chamberlain, Aristide Briand and Gustav Stresemann) regularly attended the meetings of the League Council and Assembly and played a key part in drawing up their agendas and influencing their decisions. The partnership of these three statesmen came to symbolise the new era of peace and apparent stabilisation. As long as the three European great powers cooperated, the League, too, had a chance of working.

Were these men really the great peace-makers they seemed or were they pursuing the same aims as their predecessors, although somewhat more subtly? Stresemann, particularly, is a controversial figure. Initially in the 1950s a debate raged over whether he was a great European statesman or in fact a German nationalist who just went along with Locarno as it suited Germany's interests at that point. Certainly up to 1920 Stresemann had been an uncompromising German nationalist, but in 1923 the gravity of the Ruhr crisis did convince him that only through compromise could Germany achieve the revision of Versailles and the re-establishment of its power in Europe. In a sense, as his most recent biographer, Jonathan Wright,[8] has shown, the logic of Germany's position began to push Stresemann down the road of European integration. Neither had Briand, who had threatened Germany with the occupation of the Ruhr in April 1921 (see page 55), really changed his fundamental aims. He still sought security against German aggression, but after the failure of Poincaré's Ruhr policy, he was determined to achieve it by cooperation with Britain and Germany itself. In many ways Briand was the right man for the moment. He had a genius for compromise or, as Neré has observed, 'for creating the half-light conducive to harmony'.[9] Chamberlain, too, pursued the same policies as his predecessors, but he had a much stronger hand to play. As a consequence of France's failure in the Ruhr, America's refusal to play a political role in Europe and Soviet Russia's isolation, the Dawes Plan and the Locarno Treaties made Britain the virtual arbiter between France and Germany. In that enviable but temporary position Chamberlain could simultaneously advise the Germans to be patient and the French to compromise, whilst retaining the maximum freedom for Britain to attend to the pressing problems of its empire.

After the traumas of the Depression, the collapse of the League of Nations and the Second World War the Locarno era appears in retrospect to be a brief but doomed era of hope and international progress. Most studies of this period stress the fragility and inadequacy of the stabilisation policies pursued by America and the great European powers and argue that their failure was inevitable. However, an important exception to this view is C.S. Maier's thesis that the European politicians of the late 1920s did in fact produce a viable model of stability. He argues that in retrospect 'the Depression, National Socialism and the Second World War were interruptions, albeit catastrophic ones, between a provisional political and social settlement [after Locarno] and a more permanent one [after 1945]'.[10]

# References

1 Quoted in David G. Williamson, *The British in Germany, 1918–30* (Oxford, Berg, 1991), p. 268.
2 The head of the British section of the Inter-Allied Military Control Commission to the War Office, 30 Nov. 1924, in ibid., p. 283.
3 F.S.Northedge, *The Troubled Giant*, London, Bell and Sons, 1966, p. 267
4 J. Jacobson, *Locarno Diplomacy: Germany and the West, 1925–29* (Princeton, Princeton University Press), 1972, p. 306.
5 Quoted in F.S. Northedge, *The League of Nation: Its Life and Times* (Leicester University Press, 1988), p. 196.
6 Ibid., p. 220.
7 Ibid., p. 95.
8 J. Wright, *G. Stresemann* (Oxford, OUP, 2002), p. 417.
9 J. Neré, *The Foreign Policy of France from 1914 to 1945* (London, Routledge,) 1975, p. 71.
10 C.S. Maier, *Recasting Bourgeois Europe* (Princeton, Princeton University Press, 1988 edition), p. xiii.

## Summary Diagram
The Politics of Reconciliation and Disarmament

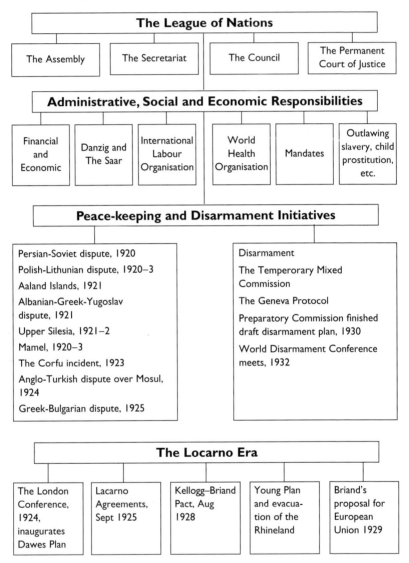

**The League of Nations**

| The Assembly | The Secretariat | The Council | The Permanent Court of Justice |

**Administrative, Social and Economic Responsibilities**

| Financial and Economic | Danzig and The Saar | International Labour Organisation | World Health Organisation | Mandates | Outlawing slavery, child prostitution, etc. |

**Peace-keeping and Disarmament Initiatives**

Persian-Soviet dispute, 1920
Polish-Lithunian dispute, 1920–3
Aaland Islands, 1921
Albanian-Greek-Yugoslav dispute, 1921
Upper Silesia, 1921–2
Mamel, 1920–3
The Corfu incident, 1923
Anglo-Turkish dispute over Mosul, 1924
Greek-Bulgarian dispute, 1925

Disarmament
The Temperorary Mixed Commission
The Geneva Protocol
Preparatory Commission finished draft disarmament plan, 1930
World Disarmament Conference meets, 1932

**The Locarno Era**

| The London Conference, 1924, inaugurates Dawes Plan | Lacarno Agreements, Sept 1925 | Kellogg–Briand Pact, Aug 1928 | Young Plan and evacuation of the Rhineland | Briand's proposal for European Union 1929 |

## Working on Chapter 4

Essentially this chapter is concerned with the improvement in international relations that took place between 1924 and 1930. Thanks to the development of the Locarno spirit, Germany was admitted into the League. The 'big European 3' could then cooperate together on the Council of the League of Nations, and they gradually began to turn the League into a real force for peace. Slowly America, too, was being drawn out of isolation. To understand this brief period of *détente* you need first of all to make sure you understand why and how the situation improved so markedly between the years 1925 and 1929. Then look carefully at all aspects of the League – its duties under Versailles, the mandate system, its social and economic work and finally its peace-keeping duties and the progress it made towards disarmament. Also analyse its constitution and make sure you understand how the League worked both in theory and in reality

## Answering structured and essay questions on Chapter 4

In preparing essay questions on this topic, it is important to bear three main themes in mind: the extent to which the peace treaties were modified by 1930, the role and effectiveness of the League of Nations 1919–30, and whether the improvement in relations between Britain, France and Germany was firmly based. Questions on all three topics appear regularly.

Look at the following structured questions:

1  a) Explain the nature of the Locarno Treaties.
   b) To what extent did they really create a new era of peace in Europe?
2  a) Explain the constitution of the League of Nations.
   b) How effective was it in achieving disarmament in the period 1920–32?

Both 1a) and 2a) are essentially factual questions aimed at testing your comprehension and knowledge. 1b) and 2b) are more complex questions. The first requires you both to analyse the international situation in Europe between 1925 and 1929 and to ask whether the intentions of Stresemann and Briand, in particular, were genuine. Did Stresemann intend just to exploit Locarno and Germany's admission to the League to regain Germany's old position or did it mark a new and more peaceful start for German foreign policy? Was Briand really ready to treat Germany as an equal or was he still after his 'pound of flesh'? 2b) is a complex and detailed question that targets the League's role in disarmament. Firstly you need to show that disarmament and the question of security went hand in hand and that on French insistence an ambitious scheme, the Geneva Protocol, was drawn up to provide worldwide security, but this failed because

Britain refused to play the role of world policeman. More progress towards disarmament was in fact made outside the League, as the conclusion of the Washington and London naval treaties and the signature of the Kellogg–Briand Pact show, because one of the most important forces pushing towards disarmament, the USA, was not a member of the League. Nevertheless the League did press on with plans for the World Disarmament Conference, but the Depression and the rise of Nazism ensured that nothing was to come of that.

The following are essay questions, which require a wider range of knowledge and more extensive answers:

1  How far by 1929 did the impact on Europe of the postwar settlements of 1919–23 disappoint the hopes of the peace-makers?
2  Had the peace settlements of 1919–23 begun to break down by 1930?
3  Why was there a mood of optimism and cooperation in Europe between 1925 and 1929 and why did it prove only temporary?
4  To what extent had the League of Nations by 1930 fulfilled the hopes it had inspired when it was founded?
5  What problems confronted the League of Nations in the years 1919–29 and to what extent was it successful in promoting the cause of peace?

In preparing these questions it will quickly become clear that you need to look back at your notes on Chapter 3. Questions 1 and 2 are both fairly straightforward and require you to discuss why the peace settlements failed, but do not forget that the examiner will expect you to be able to handle a lot of complex information in an analytical way. Above all, you must be ready to question what such statements as 'disappoint' and 'begin to break down' actually mean. Before starting such questions be sure that you really do know your facts! Both in Questions 1 and 2 you need to know the details of the postwar settlements and to what extent they were modified by the Treaty of Lausanne, Locarno and the Dawes and Young Plans. Question 3 again involves the Locarno era but also requires you to say why you think this improvement was so short-lived. Was it just the Depression that brought Hitler to power or would Franco-German relations have inevitably deteriorated as Germany recovered its strength? You will need to return to this question again after reading Chapter 5.

Questions 4 and 5 both deal with the League and invite you to construct a balance between its successes and failures. It obviously failed to make much significant progress until 1924–5, but then the cooperation between Britain, France and Germany enabled it significantly to increase its influence. Draw up a list of the League's achievements in its social and economic work as well as in its prevention of conflict in the 1920s.

## Source-based questions on Chapter 4

1 **From Dawes to Locarno, 1924–5**
Read carefully the extracts from the statement by the Treasury on pages 67–8 (Source A), Chamberlain's speech on page 70 (Source B) and Stresemann's letter to the Crown Prince on page 73 (Source C) and the photograph on page 71 (Source D). Then answer the following questions:
**a)** Study Source A
Using your own knowledge, explain briefly how this source help us understand why the government welcomed the Dawes Plan? (3 marks)
**b)** Study Source B
What is meant by 'the bones of a British Grenadier' (lines 3–4)? (2 marks)
**c)** Study all the sources and use your own knowledge
Explain how these sources help us understand British and German aims during the negotiation of the Locarno Agreements and also what their implications were for French security? (10 marks)
2 **The 'Locarno Spirit', 1925–30**
Read carefully Briand's speech to the Assembly of the League of Nations on page 75 (Source A) and the clauses of the Kellogg–Briand Pact on page 87 (Source B), and then study the cartoon on page 72 (Source C). Answer the following questions:
**a)** Study Source A
What does Source A reveal about the aims of French foreign policy? (5 marks)
**b)** Study Source B
Explain the meaning of Point 2 of the Kellogg–Briand Pact (lines 5–8). (2 marks)
**c)** Study Source C
What is the significance of the empty cupboard in the cartoon? (3 marks)
**d)** Study all the Sources and use your own knowledge
Consider whether the cartoonist's prediction was confirmed by international developments between 1925 and 1930. (10 marks)
3 **The work of the League of Nations**
Carefully read the extract from the British commentary on page 78 (Source A), Article 16 on page 80 (Source B), the remark by a French delegate to the League Assembly on page 83 (Source C), the extract from Briand's speech of October 1925 to the Council of the League on page 85 (Source D), Article 22 of the League constitution on page 81 (Source E) and Professor Zimmern's commentary on page 82 (Source F). Answer the following questions:
**a)** Study Source A
What does the British official commentary mean by 'trust in the influence of custom to mould opinion' (lines 4–5)? (2 marks)

**b)** Study Source E
Explain what is meant in Article 22 by 'peoples not yet able to stand by themselves under the strenuous conditions of the modern world' (lines 3–5). (*2 marks*)

**c)** Study sources A, B and C and use your own knowledge
Do sources A and C agree on the potential ineffectiveness of Article 16? (Source B) (*6 marks*)

**d)** Study all the sources and use your own knowledge.
Do you agree that the League was a success in the 1920s? (*20 marks*)

Source-based questions usually test comprehension, comparison and/or corroboration and the use of your own knowledge to explain and develop the facts and arguments in the sources. As comprehension questions test your knowledge of the details of the period you have studied, the only way you can be sure to gain full marks is to make sure you know them well. Sometimes examiners ask you to make direct comparisons between documents, but an equally popular format is: 'To what extent do sources x and y support the view that ...' or 'do they agree on ...?' The one thing **not** to do when comparing sources is to summarise first one source and then another, while leaving the crucial comparison to a small last paragraph. Approach a comparison question thematically and start comparing straight away. Remember that comparisons are concerned with both similarities and dissimilarities. When you are asked to study the sources and use your own knowledge, you have to achieve a balance between your own knowledge and the documents. If you miss out on either of them, the examiner cannot give you much above 50%.

# 5 The Impact of the Great Depression on International Politics

## POINTS TO CONSIDER

As you read through this chapter it is important to identify how the Depression unleashed forces that destroyed the peace settlement of 1919. One the one hand, it drove the USA back into isolation and weakened first Britain and then France, so that they were reluctant to rearm and take a leading role in supporting the League. On the other hand, it also provided the context for the take-over of power by Hitler and the seizure of Manchuria by the Japanese army. A vital question to consider is why Britain and France were unable to contain Nazi Germany and Japan. The impact of the Depression is one reason, but as you read through the chapter, you may come to the conclusion that lack of unity amongst the former victorious powers in the years 1930–5 was also important, as was the disastrous mishandling of the Abyssinian crisis.

## KEY DATES

| | | |
|---|---|---|
| **1931** | March | German proposal for customs union with Austria |
| **1932** | February | Disarmament Conference met at Geneva |
| | July | Lausanne conference: Reparations virtually abolished |
| | September | Mukden incident |
| **1933** | 30 January | Hitler appointed Chancellor of Germany |
| | February | Japan left League of Nations |
| | October | Germany left both League and Disarmament Conference |
| **1934** | January | German-Polish non-Aggression Pact |
| | July | Nazi uprising in Austria failed |
| **1935** | January | Saar plebiscite |
| | March | Hitler reintroduced conscription |
| | April | Stresa Front |
| | May | Franco-Soviet Pact |
| | June | Anglo-German Naval Agreement |
| | October | Abyssinia invaded by Italy |
| **1936** | March | Rhineland re-militarized |
| | July | Spanish Civil war starts |
| | October | Rome–Berlin Axis |
| | November | Anti-Comintern Pact |

# 1 The Great Depression

> **KEY ISSUES** How did the Great Depression weaken the economies of the great powers, and how did the measures that they took to protect their economies influence the international situation?

The Great Depression, triggered by the Wall Street Crash, marked a turning point in interwar history. Not only did it weaken the economic and social stability of the world's major powers, but it also dealt a devastating blow to the progress made since 1924 towards creating a new framework for peaceful international cooperation. It has been called by Robert Boyce 'the third global catastrophe of the century'[1] (along with the two world wars). It is hard to exaggerate its international impact. To a great extent the economic recovery in Europe after 1924 had been dependent on short-term American loans, of which, for instance, $4 billion went to Germany. After the Wall Street stock exchange crash, American investors abruptly terminated these loans and no more were forthcoming – a devastating blow to the European and world economies. Between 1929 and 1932 the volume of world trade fell by 70%. Unemployment rose to 13 million in the USA, to 6 million in Germany and to 3 million in Britain. Japan was particularly hard hit: some 50% of its mining and heavy industrial capacity was forced to close and the collapse of the American market virtually destroyed its large and lucrative export trade in silk.

Inevitably an economic crisis on this scale had a decisive political impact. In Germany it ultimately brought Hitler to power and in Japan it strengthened the hand of an influential group of army officers who argued that only by seizing Manchuria could Japan recover from the slump. In Italy it prompted Mussolini to have plans drawn up for the conquest of Abyssinia. The Depression's impact on the politics of the three democracies was equally disastrous. It delayed their rearmament programmes and created an international climate in which each of the three suspected the others of causing its financial and economic difficulties. It thus prevented any effective collaboration between them at a time when it was vital both to deter the aggressive nationalism of Japan and Germany and to deal with the global economic crisis.

As international trade collapsed, the great powers erected tariff barriers and attempted to make themselves economically self-sufficient. The British and the French with their huge colonial empires had a decisive advantage over the Germans, Italians and Japanese, who increasingly began to assert their right to carve out their own empires, spheres of interest or 'Lebensraum' (living space) as Hitler called it. The Depression encouraged a dangerously competitive nationalism that was neatly summed up in 1936 by Hitler in 'The Four Year Plan Memorandum': 'Politics is the conduct and the course of the historical struggle for life. The aim of these struggles is survival'.

# 2 The Manchurian Crisis

> **KEY ISSUES**  Why did Japan occupy Manchuria and why was the
> League of nations unable to prevent it?

Arguably, the Japanese occupation of Manchuria in 1931 was a continuation of policies followed by Japanese governments since the
defeat of Russia in 1905 when Japan had been awarded the lease of
the South Manchurian Railway and the right to protect it with some
15,000 troops. In the late 1920s these concessions were threatened by
the course of the Chinese civil war. In 1928 Chiang Kai-shek, the
leader of the Chinese Nationalists, had occupied Beijing. The Japanese
army feared that the local Chinese War Lord, who controlled most of
Manchuria, would rally to Chiang Kai-shek and began to draw up
plans to strengthen its hold on the province. Initially the Tokyo
government was strong enough to restrain the army. However, its
weakness in the face of the onset of the Depression strengthened its
critics, amongst whom both the officer corps and the patriotic societies played a major role. In November 1930 the Japanese Prime
Minister was wounded in an attempted assassination by a member of
one of the patriotic societies, and in the following March plans, which
were only cancelled at the last moment, were drawn up for a military
coup.

The weak government at home together with the consequences
of the Depression convinced the army both in Manchuria and at
home that it would have to act decisively and occupy the whole of
Manchuria. This would then enable Japan to control the region's
valuable coal and iron resources of at a time when economic pro-
tectionism was already making it difficult for it to purchase these
vital raw materials elsewhere. Consequently Japanese officers in
Manchuria decided to devise an incident that would provide the pretext for it to act. On 18 September 1931 a bomb exploded on the railway line just outside Mukden where both local Chinese and Japanese
troops were stationed. This was immediately blamed on the Chinese
and provided the Japanese forces with the desired excuse to occupy
not only Mukden but the whole of southern Manchuria. China
immediately appealed to the League of Nations, but the Council
responded cautiously. It first asked Japan to withdraw its troops back
into the railway zone and then, when this was ignored, sent a commission of enquiry under the chairmanship of Lord Lytton. The
Japanese completed the occupation of Manchuria and turned it into
the satellite state of Manchukuo while the Lytton Commission was
conducting a leisurely fact-finding operation in the spring of 1932.

It is easy to criticise the League for not acting more decisively, but
without the commitment of the great powers it was not in the position
to take effective action. Neither of the two most important naval
powers, Britain and the USA, was ready to use force against Japan.

From the Japanese point of view, the timing of the Mukden incident could not have been better. On 15 September a minor mutiny at the naval base at Invergordon, which was caused by a cut in the sailors' wages, threatened temporarily to paralyse the Royal Navy; and 5 days later Britain was forced off the gold standard. America, shell-shocked by the Depression, was unwilling to do more than denounce Japanese aggression. President Hoover argued that economic sanctions would be like 'sticking pins in tigers'[2] and would run the risk of leading to war. It is sometimes argued that the British government and powerful financial interests in the City of London secretly supported Japan. It is true that Britain did have some sympathy with Japanese action in Manchuria. Like Japan it had commercial interests in China which it felt were threatened by the chaos and civil war there. Britain also appreciated Japan's potential role in providing a barrier against the spread of Bolshevism from Russia into northern China. Nevertheless, the real reason why Britain was not ready to urge more decisive action against Japan was that neither its government nor its people desired to fight a war on an issue that was not central to British interests. In February 1933 Sir John Simon, the Foreign Minister, told the House of Commons:

i   I think I am myself enough of a pacifist to take the view that however
    we handle the matter, I do not intend my own country to get into
    trouble about it  There is one great difference between 1914 and now
    and it is this: in no circumstances will this Government authorise this
5   country to be party to this struggle.

It was not until September that the League received the Commission's report. Although it accepted that the treaty rights, which Japan had enjoyed in Manchuria since 1905 had intensified Sino-Japanese friction, it nevertheless emphasised that

> without a declaration of war a large area of what was indisputably
> Chinese territory had been forcibly seized and occupied by the armed
> forces of Japan and has in consequence of this operation been separ-
> ated from and declared independent of the rest of China.

The Commission stressed that the problem of Manchuria could only be solved by a general improvement in Sino-Japanese relations and proposed that, after Japanese troops had been withdrawn back into the railway zone, both China and Japan should negotiate not only a treaty guaranteeing Japan's rights in Manchuria but also a non-aggression pact and a trade agreement. Essentially then the report was mistakenly based on the assumption that the Japanese had no territorial designs in China and were ready to compromise over Manchuria. When it was adopted unanimously, with the single exception of Japan, by the League Assembly on 24 February 1933, Japan withdrew from the League in protest. It was obvious that only armed intervention by the great powers would now be able to force it out of Manchuria, and that option was not politically realistic in 1933.

The Japanese occupation of Manchuria changed the balance of power in the Pacific. Japan had broken free from the restraints imposed upon it at the Washington Conference in 1922 by Britain and America (see page 86) and had guaranteed its access to valuable coal and iron ore resources. Above all Japan was now in a favourable strategic position to plan a large-scale military invasion of China. The Manchurian incident is often seen as the first link in a chain of events that led to the Second World War. Later a Liberal British MP, Sir Geoffrey Mander, argued that the 'pathway to the beaches of Dunkirk lay through the waste of Manchuria'.[3] However, although it did weaken the League and the whole idea of collective security, it did not necessarily signal the end of the Versailles system in Europe or the end of the League's peace-keeping role. The Abyssinian crisis (see pages 108–11) was to play a far more important part in its destruction.

# 3  German Foreign Policy, 1930–5

Were there continuities in German foreign policy between 1930 and 1935? What were the aims of Nazi foreign policy and what had Hitler achieved by 1935?

## a) The Foreign Policy of Brüning, Papen and Schleicher

In March 1930 Heinrich Brüning was appointed Chancellor of a minority government supported by the German Nationalists. Only months after the acceptance of the Young Plan (see page 75), he was determined not only to end reparation payments but also to assert Germany's right to rearm and to free itself from the remaining restrictions of the Treaty of Versailles. Brüning and his two successors, Papen and Schleicher, created what J.W. Hiden has called 'the diplomatic-military instruments which Hitler was able to use in the early stages of his regime'.[4] Hitler was able to reassure the European powers and his own diplomats, at least until 1935, that he was only following the revisionist policies of his immediate predecessors.

In the summer of 1930 Brüning seized upon proposals first put forward by the Austrian government for a customs union with Germany, arguing that Germany needed 'an adequate natural area of living space'.[5] The plan was opposed bitterly by the French who feared that a customs union would inevitably lead to a political union, which was contrary to both the Treaties of St Germain and Versailles. Thus, when Germany was plunged into a major banking crisis triggered by the collapse of the Darmstadt and National Bank, the French blocked every proposal for an emergency loan until Germany not only renounced the customs union but also abandoned attempts to revise reparations for at least 5 years. Nevertheless, the sheer scale of the banking crisis helped Brüning ultimately achieve his overriding aim of abolishing reparations. In July 1931 a proposal put forward by President Hoover for a year's moratorium on all international debts was accepted by the great powers. Brüning skillfully used this year to convince the Americans and British that the payment of reparations was no longer a realistic option by stressing both Germany's financial weakness and the strength of nationalist opposition to it. He was largely successful, although he was forced to resign a month before the powers agreed at the Lausanne Conference in June 1932 effectively to cancel reparations altogether.

At the World Disarmament Conference, which first met in February 1932, the time was again right for a determined German initiative. The western democracies were divided and uncertain. The French had an ambitious programme for allocating national forces to a League police force for peace-keeping operations, while America and Britain viewed this potentially open-ended commitment with alarm. Brüning insisted on Germany achieving equality of armaments with the other major European powers, either by them disarming down to the German level or by allowing Germany to rearm up to theirs. That he was really thinking of the latter solution was shown by his proposals for doubling the Germany army. After months of heated debate and a German threat to walk out of the conference, a face-saving formula was devised whereby Germany's 'equality of rights would be recognised within 'a system which would provide security for all nations'.[5] Significantly, in November 1932, the German War Ministry finalised a plan for large increases in the army, which were to be achieved by 1938.

## b) Hitler

The tempo of the German campaign against Versailles quickened once Hitler came to power in 1933, although for 2 years, at least, he appeared to pursue the same policy as Brüning, albeit somewhat more vigorously and unconventionally. Was he then just following the traditional policy of making Germany 'the greatest power in Europe from her natural weight by exploiting every opportunity that presented itself', as A.J.P. Taylor argued?[7]

In his book, *Mein Kampf*, written in 1924, Hitler was quite specific about the main thrust of Nazi foreign policy:

1  And so we National Socialists consciously draw a line beneath the foreign policy tendency of our prewar period. We take up where we broke off six hundred years ago. We stop the endless German movement to the south and west and turn our gaze towards the land in the
5  east. At long last we break off the colonial and commercial policy of the prewar period and shift to the soil policy of the future. If we speak of soil in Europe, we can primarily have in mind only Russia and her vassal border states.

Was this still an aim in 1933 or was it just a pipe-dream long since forgotten? Like Taylor, Hans Mommsen doubts whether Hitler had a consistent foreign policy of 'unchanging … priorities'[8] and argues that it was usually determined by economic pressures and demands for action from within the Nazi Party itself. Other historians, particularly those of the 'Programme School',[9] take a diametrically opposed line and argue on the strength of *Mein Kampf* and *Hitler's Secret Book* (published in 1928) that he had a definite programme. First of all he planned to defeat France and Russia, and then, after building up a large navy, make a determined bid for world power, even if it involved war against both Britain and the USA. The history of Nazi foreign policy generates such controversy because Hitler's actions were so often ambiguous and contradictory. Despite this, there is currently a general consensus among historians that Hitler did intend to wage a series of wars which would ultimately culminate in a struggle for global hegemony. As Alan Bullock has argued, the key to understanding Hitler's foreign policy is that he combined 'consistency of aim with complete opportunism in method and tactics'.[10]

In 1933 Hitler's immediate priorities were to consolidate the Nazi take-over of power and to re-build Germany's military strength. This would eventually put him in a position to destroy what remained of the Versailles system. However, whilst rearming, he had to be careful not to provoke an international backlash. He therefore followed a cautious policy of avoiding risks and defusing potential opposition, while gradually withdrawing Germany from any multilateral commitments, such as being a member of the League of Nations, which might prevent him from pursuing an independent policy. He hoped particularly to isolate France by negotiating alliances with Britain and Italy. His immediate aim was to extricate Germany from the World Disarmament Conference, but he was careful to wait until the autumn before he risked withdrawing from both the Conference and the League of Nations. He had first skilfully reassured Britain and Italy of his peaceful intentions by signing in June 1933 the Four Power Pact, proposed by Mussolini, which aimed at revising Versailles through joint agreement of the great powers. Although on the face of it this seemed to limit Germany's freedom of action, Hitler calculated, correctly as it turned out, that the French would never ratify it.

Hitler's first major initiative in foreign policy was the conclusion of the German–Polish Non-aggression Pact. He did this despite opposition from the German Foreign Office, which wanted to maintain good relations with Soviet Russia. This seriously weakened France's security system in eastern Europe, as it had relied upon its alliance with Poland to put pressure on Germany's eastern frontiers. Nevertheless, Germany still remained very vulnerable. Hitler was warned in August 1934 by a senior German diplomat, B.W. von Bülow, that:

| In judging the situation we should never overlook the fact that no kind of rearmament in the next few years could give us military security.

> Even apart from our isolation, we shall for a long time yet be hopelessly
> inferior to France in the military sphere. A particularly dangerous
> 5 period will be 1934–5 on account of the re-organisation of the
> *Reichswehr* [Army].

Hitler was certainly aware of this danger, but over Austria he adopted a more provocative line, possibly because he assumed that Austria was a domestic German affair. In June 1934 he met Mussolini at Venice and tried to convince him that Austria should become a German satellite. When Mussolini rejected this, Hitler gave the Austrian Nazis strong unofficial encouragement to stage a month later what turned out to be a disastrously unsuccessful uprising in Vienna. Mussolini, determined to keep Austria as a buffer state between Italy and Germany, immediately mobilised troops on the Brenner frontier and forced Hitler to disown the coup. The incident brought about a sharp deterioration in German-Italian relations and appeared to rule out any prospect of an alliance.

In March 1935 Hitler took another risk when he announced the re-introduction of conscription, despite the fears of his advisers that this would lead to French intervention. Initially these fears appeared to be confirmed when in April the British, French and Italian heads of government met at Stresa and both condemned German rearmament and resolved to maintain the peace settlements. Hitler, however, quickly launched a diplomatic offensive to reassure the powers of his peaceful intentions. In a speech that in places appeared to echo the language of Stresemann and Briand he proposed a series of non-aggression pacts with Germany's neighbours, promised to observe Locarno and accept an over-all limitation on armaments. He also offered Britain an agreement limiting the German fleet to 35% of the total strength of the Royal Navy. He concluded with an apparently deep commitment to peace and reconstruction:

> 1 Whoever lights the torch of war in Europe can wish for nothing but
> chaos. We, however, can live in the firm conviction that in our time will
> be fulfilled, not the decline, but the renaissance of the West. That
> Germany may make an imperishable contribution to this great work is
> 5 our proud hope and unshakable belief.

His tactics were partly successful. Britain did rise to the bait and accept Hitler's terms for an Anglo-German Naval Convention in June 1935. This appeared to give British approval to German rearmament and broke up the unity of the Stresa Front. On the other hand, there were signs in the summer of 1935 that France's efforts to contain Germany were beginning to be successful. France was able to exploit Mussolini's opposition to Hitler's ambitions in Austria to negotiate a Franco-Italian agreement in January 1935. By June the armies of two powers were already beginning to consider how they could cooperate in the event of war against Germany, while on 2 May the Franco-Russian Pact was signed (see pages 104–5).

# 4 The Reaction of the Great Powers to Nazi Germany, 1933–5

> **KEY ISSUE** How did the great powers adapt to Hitler's efforts to restore the power of Germany, 1933–5?

For the great powers 1933–5 was a period in which they had to come to terms with the reality of Nazi Germany. In 1933, even though Germany was only just beginning to rearm, its strength was potentially far greater than in 1914, as it was enhanced by a ring of weak states which had been created in 1919 out of the ruins of the Austrian and Russian empires around its eastern and southern frontiers.

## a) France

By 1934 France had long since lost the diplomatic leadership of Europe which it had exercised in the immediate postwar years. Its economy had been belatedly hit by the Depression and its social cohesion threatened by a wave of rioting sparked off in February 1934 by the exposure of a series of financial scandals. Even if it had still possessed the will to intervene militarily in Germany, the Locarno Treaties prevented it from reoccupying the Rhineland. Neither could it rely on Poland after the Polish–German Non-aggression Pact of January 1934. France's response to the new Nazi Germany was therefore hesitant and sometimes contradictory. It sought to contain Germany, as it had done since 1919, through a network of alliances and pacts but, like Britain, it also tried to negotiate with Hitler.

Although ultimately Britain remained France's major European partner, it continued to remain aloof from Continental entanglements until 1939. French alliance policy was therefore primarily aimed at strengthening the Little *Entente* and negotiating agreements with Italy and Russia. However, this was by no means an easy task as in 1933 its relations with both powers were strained. The French were suspicious of the long-standing Italian ambitions in the Balkans and North Africa and were irritated by Mussolini's tendency to side with the Germans at the Disarmament Conference. Nevertheless, from the summer of 1933 onwards the French launched a major initiative to negotiate an Italian alliance, which they believed was crucial in stabilising the Balkans and containing Germany. In this they were greatly helped by the abortive Nazi coup in Vienna, which more than anything convinced Mussolini that cooperation with France was essential.

In January 1935 both countries signed the Rome Agreements by which they undertook not to meddle in the affairs of their Balkan neighbours and to act together in the event of unilateral German rearmament or another threat to Austrian independence. Italy's new orientation towards Paris appeared to be confirmed when Britain, France and Italy met at Stresa in April 1935 to condemn German rearmament. While historians have tended to dismiss the Stresa Declarations as mere platitudes, the meeting did nevertheless lead on in June to direct Franco-Italian military staff talks to discuss joint action in the event of a German attack on Austria, Italy or France.

Parallel with these negotiations, talks were proceeding between the French and the Russians. Paris did not show the same enthusiasm for a Russian alliance as it did for one with Italy. This was partly because Soviet Russia had been regarded as scarcely less of a threat to the West than Germany and partly because it no longer had a common border with Germany. In November 1932 the French government had signed a non-aggression pact with Russia, but when in the summer of 1933 the Russians proposed a more ambitious 'secret verbal agreement' on political cooperation, the first reaction of the French was to question Russia's motives. Paul-Boncour, the French Foreign Minister, observed:

> By appearing ... to consider only Germany, and the pursuit of European agreements which would be likely to coincide with our views, is not the USSR really concerned most of all with Japan and prompted by the ulterior motive of committing us in Asia?

Nevertheless, there were compelling reasons to respond positively to Russia's initiatives, as the French ambassador in Moscow reminded his government in September 1933:

1 After a failure of the British and American agreements of the Treaty of Versailles and ... in the middle of the difficulties in which the British Empire and the United States are struggling, which make concrete undertakings with regard to European affairs more and more unlikely,
5 this is ... a system based on agreement with the USSR ... which in present circumstances may guarantee French security.

By April 1934, after the shock of the German–Polish Non-aggression Pact, the French were ready to renew negotiations with Russia. However, they aimed to enmesh Soviet Russia in an elaborate treaty of regional assistance or, in other words, an eastern European version of the Locarno Treaty, which would be signed not only by Russia but also by Germany, Poland, Czechoslovakia and the Baltic States. This was to be buttressed by a separate Franco-Russian agreement which would associate Russia with the Locarno Agreements in western Europe (see pages 70–1) and France with the proposed eastern pact. But the whole plan came to nothing as both Germany and Poland refused to join. The Poles were more suspicious of the Russians than of the Germans. France had therefore little option but to pursue a mutual assistance pact with Soviet Russia alone. The final impetus to its negotiation was given by Germany's introduction of conscription in March 1935. By May the Pact had been signed. Even then the French did not quite overcome their suspicions of Soviet Russia. They refused to follow up the pact with detailed military staff talks between the two armies. For them it was sufficient that the pact should restrain Russia from moving closer to Germany, as it had done in 1922 when it had signed the Rapallo Agreement (see page 56).

Meanwhile the French government attempted to negotiate a settlement with Germany. Both in the winter of 1933–4 and in the summer of 1935, immediately after the signature of the Franco-Soviet Treaty, attempts were made to begin a Franco-German dialogue. These efforts were doomed as the French attempted to draw the Germans into negotiating agreements essentially aimed at preserving the Versailles system. Hitler was ready, when it suited him, to lower the political temperature through cordial diplomatic exchanges, but he was not ready to tolerate the restrictions with which French – and British – diplomacy was attempting to entangle him.

## b) Great Britain

The British government had no illusions about the potential danger from Germany. As early as 1934 Neville Chamberlain, then Chancellor of the Exchequer, described Germany as the '*fons et origo* [fount and origin] of all our European troubles and anxieties'.[11] Like France, Britain's reaction to Nazi Germany was conditioned by its military, economic and strategic vulnerability. In 1933 it faced not only a growing threat from Germany in Europe, but also from Japan in the Far East. By the autumn of 1935 when Italy invaded Abyssinia, this danger was further compounded by possible threats from Italian naval forces to its Mediterranean position. That year the Government's Defence Requirement Committee warned that:

1  It is a cardinal [fundamental] requirement of our national and imperial security that our foreign policy should be conducted so as to avoid the possible development of a situation in which we might be confronted simultaneously with the hostility of Japan in the Far East, Germany in
5  the West and any power on the main line of communication between the two.

Consequently, the main aim of British policy towards Germany was to blunt Hitler's aggression by continuing to modify the Treaty of Versailles while simultaneously drawing Germany back into the League where it could be tied down in multilateral agreements on security. Sir John Simon, the Foreign minister, summed up this policy in a letter to King George V in February 1935:

1  The practical choice is between a Germany which continues to rearm without any regulation or agreement and a Germany which through getting a recognition of its rights and some modification of the Peace

Treaties, enters into the comity of nations and contributes, in this and
5 other ways, to European stability.

Britain supported any initiative which appeared to lead to the pacifi-
cation of Europe within the overall structure created by the peace
treaties of 1919–20, such as Mussolini's proposal for a four-power pact
in 1933, the French plans for an eastern Locarno or the German
Polish Non-aggression Treaty, which the Foreign Office believed
thawed the 'cold war' that had been a feature of relations between
Warsaw and Berlin since 1919 (see page 77). Britain also worked hard
for an overall settlement with Germany. Despite the reintroduction of
German conscription in March, Sir John Simon went to Berlin later
in the month to explore the possibility of a comprehensive settlement
with Germany involving German recognition of Austrian independence, its participation in an 'eastern Locarno' and return to the
League. British ministers attended the Stresa meeting on 8 April, but
they were determined not to be manoeuvred into an anti-German
front. In the Cabinet on 8 April:

1  a suggestion was very generally supported that, if asked by France and
   Italy to put an end to conversations with Germany and to do nothing
   more than indicate our intention to stand firm with France and Italy, we
   should not agree to it. Our line, therefore, it was suggested, should be
5  that we could not agree to make a complete breach with Germany, and
   to take no action to threaten her

The British government was not at that stage ready to join any
alliances or pacts directed against Germany as it was convinced that
the pre-1914 alliance system had been a major cause of the very war it
was aimed to prevent. In June this policy seemed to be rewarded with
success when the Anglo-German Naval Agreement was signed.

## c) Italy

Mussolini, who had his own extensive revisionist and imperialist programme which he intended to implement in the Balkans and North
Africa, at first attempted to maintain a special position as mediator
between Germany on the one hand and Britain and France on the
other. He thus hoped that his proposed Four-Power Pact of June 1933
(see page 101) would enable Italy to play a major part in Europe and
take a lead in revising those parts of the Treaty of Versailles it disliked.
However, French scepticism towards the Pact and the increasing
German threat to Austria began to convert Mussolini from a critic and
potential revisionist of the Treaty of Versailles to an upholder of the
territorial status quo. As early as August 1933 Mussolini met Dollfuss,
the Austrian Chancellor, at Rimini and discussed arrangements for
Italian military support in case of German intervention in Austria. In
March 1934 he further strengthened his position against Germany by

negotiating the Rome Protocols with Austria and Hungary which provided for diplomatic consultations should any of the three powers call for them. Mussolini's conversion to a defender of the existing territorial settlement was accelerated by the abortive Nazi putsch in Vienna in July 1934 and by the German announcement of conscription the following March. The Rome Agreements of January 1935 were, as we have seen, a triumph for French policy, but they were also significant because they marked France's recognition of Italy as a great power in its own right. Mussolini attempted to fulfil this role by taking the lead in orchestrating opposition to German rearmament when he invited Britain and France to the Stresa Conference in April 1935. By the spring of 1935, therefore, Italy appeared to have aligned itself firmly with Britain and France in their desire to preserve what was left of the Versailles settlement.

## d) Soviet Russia

Like Mussolini, but for different reasons, Stalin was becoming increasingly conservative in his approach to foreign policy issues and was ever more anxious to preserve the status quo. This was not only because Russia was threatened in the Far East by Japan, but also because it was particularly vulnerable to attack while it was going through the immense internal upheavals caused by the collectivisation programme, which was a ruthless attempt to force millions of peasants into collective or state-run farms. Stalin, like the other European leaders, reacted cautiously to the Nazi take-over of power. He was not sure how long Hitler would remain in power. In 1930 he had ordered the German Communist Party not to cooperate with the SPD, the German Socialist Party, on the grounds that a victory of the Nazis, whom he thought were the puppets of the great industrialists, would lead to a German Communist revolution. Even if this were not to happen, he hoped that the traditions of the Rapallo policy and a common hatred of Poland would ensure the continuation of Soviet–German cooperation. His distrust of the West was at least as great as his fear of Nazi Germany. At the seventeenth congress of the Russian Communist Party in 1934 he observed:

1  Some politicians say that the USSR has now taken an orientation towards France and Poland; that from an opponent of the Versailles Treaty it has become a supporter of that treaty, and that this change is to be explained by the establishment of the Fascist regime in Germany.
5  That is not true. Of course, we are far from being enthusiastic about the Fascist regime in Germany. But Fascism is not the issue here, if only for the reason that Fascism in Italy, for instance, has not prevented the USSR from establishing the best relations with that country.

Stalin, like the French and British governments, tried both to strengthen his defences against Germany and to reassure Hitler.

While discussing possible security pacts with the French and joining the League of Nations in September 1934, he attempted to maintain good relations with Germany despite such setbacks as the German–Polish Non-aggression Pact (see page 101). In 1934, for instance, Russia repaid most of the loans it had borrowed from Germany and proposed to Hitler a joint agreement guaranteeing the independence of the Baltic states. The Russian negotiations with the French in the spring of 1935 were also accompanied by a series of secret talks with the Germans, which mirrored the French tactics of trying for a settlement with Hitler in the summer of 1935 (see page 105) as an alternative to the Franco–Soviet Pact. Soviet–Nazi talks continued intermittently right up to February 1936. Only with the ratification of the Pact by the French parliament were they finally broken off.

## e) The USA

In 1933 there was considerable sympathy in America for postwar republican Germany, while both Britain and France were viewed with some suspicion on account of their huge colonial empires. However, Nazi Germany rapidly increased hostility in the USA through such ideological actions as the persecution of the Jews. But, in the short term, mounting popular irritation with Nazi Germany was insufficient to influence the foreign policy of the American government, which was determined to keep clear of any European entanglements. Similarly in the Far East the USA was alarmed by the Japanese occupation of Manchuria, but did no more than make diplomatic protest (see page 98). Indeed, the Temporary Neutrality Act of 1935, by empowering the President to ban the supply of arms to all belligerents – whether aggressors or victims of aggression – in the event of the outbreak of war, strengthened this policy of non-involvement.

## 5 The Abyssinian Crisis

> **KEY ISSUE** Why was the conquest of Abyssinia not stopped by Britain and France?

Mussolini had for a long time wanted to build up a large empire in North Africa which would have the added advantage of distracting his people from the impact of the Depression on the Italian economy. By 1932 he had begun to plan in earnest the annexation of Abyssinia. Not only would Abyssinia provide land for Italian settlers, but it would also connect Eritrea with Italian Somaliland and thus put most of the Horn of Africa under Italian control. In December 1934 a clash occurred between Italian and Abyssinian troops at the small oasis of

Wal-Wal, some 50 miles on the Abyssinian side of the border with Italian Somaliland. The following October the long expected invasion of Abyssinia began. Mussolini was convinced that neither Britain nor France would raise serious objections. In January 1935 Laval, the French Foreign Minister, had verbally promised him a free hand, while the British Foreign Office was desperate to avert the crisis either by offering Mussolini territorial compensation elsewhere or by helping to negotiate an arrangement, comparable to Britain's own position in Egypt, which would give Italy effective control of Abyssinia without formal annexation. Sir Robert Vansittart, a senior British diplomat, forcefully pointed out that:

1  The position is as plain as a pikestaff. Italy will have to be bought off – let us use and face ugly words – in some form or other, or Abyssinia will eventually perish. That might in itself matter less, if it did not mean that the League would also perish (and that Italy would simultaneously
5  perform another *volte-face* [about turn] into the arms of Germany).

Why then could such a compromise not be negotiated? The scale and brutality of the Italian invasion confronted both the British and

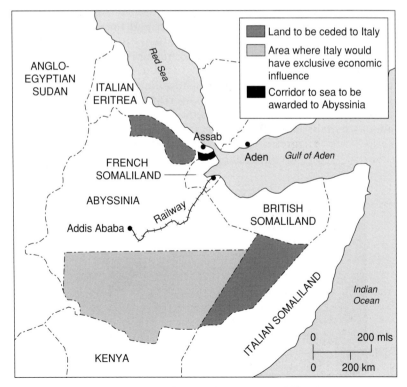

The Hoare–Laval Plan for the partition of Abyssinia

French governments with a considerable dilemma. The British government was facing an election in November 1935 and was under intense pressure from the electorate to support the League. In an unofficial peace ballot organised by the League of Nations Union in June 1935, 10 out of 11 million replies backed the use of economic sanctions by the League in a case of aggression. In France public opinion was more divided, with the Left supporting the League and the Right supporting Italy. However, both powers feared the diplomatic consequences of alienating Italy over Abyssinia. In particular, Britain's persistent refusal to join France in guaranteeing the status quo in central and eastern Europe inevitably increased the importance for the French of their friendly relations with Italy.

On 18 October the League condemned Italian action and voted for a gradually escalating programme of sanctions. In the meantime both Britain and France continued to search for a compromise settlement. In December Laval and the British Foreign Minister, Sir Samuel Hoare, produced a plan which had in fact already been discussed by the League in September. It involved effectively placing some two-thirds of Abyssinia under Italian control. There was a strong possibility that it would have been acceptable to Mussolini, but it was leaked to the French press and an explosion of rage amongst the British public forced Hoare's resignation and the dropping of the plan. The failure of diplomacy did not then ensure vigorous action against Mussolini. The League put no embargo on oil exports to Italy, and Britain refused to close the Suez Canal to Italian shipping on the grounds that this might lead to war. Mussolini was thus able to step up his campaign and by May 1936 had overrun Abyssinia.

Britain and France had gained the worst of all worlds. They had alienated Italy and failed to deter future aggressors by using the

*The Girls He Left Behind,* David Low cartoon.

League as an effective institution for enforcing collective security. The only power to benefit immediately from the crisis was Germany. In this sense the Abyssinian crisis rather than the Manchurian crisis was indeed the crucial turning point in the 1930s. Not only did it irreparably weaken the League and provide Hitler with an ideal opportunity for the illegal remilitarisation of the Rhineland (see below), but it also effectively destroyed the Franco-Italian friendship and ultimately replaced it with the Rome–Berlin 'Axis'. This eventually enabled Hitler in 1938 to absorb Austria without Italian opposition. The 'Axis' was also to threaten vital British and French lines of communication in the Mediterranean with the possibility of hostile naval action and thus seriously weaken their potential response to future German – or indeed Japanese – aggression.

# 6 The Remilitarisation of the Rhineland

> **KEY ISSUE**  Why, despite the Locarno Agreements, was there no effective opposition when Hitler broke the Treaty of Versailles and remilitarised the Rhineland? What were the consequences of this?

The remilitarisation of the Rhineland marked an important stage in Hitler's plans for rebuilding German power. The construction of strong fortifications there would enable him to stop any French attempts to invade Germany. Hitler had originally planned to reoccupy the Rhineland in 1937, but a combination of the favourable diplomatic situation created by the Abyssinian crisis and the need to distract domestic attention from German economic problems brought about by the speed of the rearmament programme, persuaded him to act in March 1936. In December 1935 the German Army was ordered to start planning the reoccupation, while Hitler's diplomats began to manufacture a legal justification for such action by arguing that the Franco-Soviet Pact was contrary to the Locarno Agreement. Crucial to the success of his plan was the attitude of Italy. Mussolini, isolated from the other Stresa powers because of his Abyssinian policy, had little option but to reassure Germany that he would not cooperate with the British and French to enforce Locarno if German troops entered the Rhineland.

German troops marched into the Rhineland on 7 March 1936. In order to reassure France that they did not intend to violate the Franco-German frontier they were initially, at any rate, few in number and lightly equipped. Why then did the French army not immediately intervene? The French General Staff, which since the late 1920s had been planning for a defensive war against Germany based on the fortifications of the Maginot line (named after André Maginot, the French

Minister of Defence) on France's eastern frontier, refused to agree to an invasion of the Rhineland unless France had full backing from the British. The most the British government was ready to do was to promise France that in the event of an unprovoked German attack on French territory it would send two divisions of troops across the Channel. Essentially British public opinion was convinced that Hitler was merely walking into 'his own back garden'. Hugh Dalton, the Labour shadow Foreign Secretary, emphasised in the Commons on 26 March that:

> it is only right to say bluntly and frankly that public opinion in this country would not support ... the taking of military sanctions or even of economic sanctions against Germany at this time in order to put German troops out of the Rhineland.

The demilitarisation of the Rhineland was a triumph for Hitler, and, as an internal French Foreign Office memorandum of 12 March 1936 stressed, it marked a decisive shift in power from Paris to Berlin:

> 1 A German success would likewise not fail to encourage elements which, in Yugoslavia, look towards Berlin ... In Rumania this will be a victory of the elements of the Right which have been stirred up by Hitlerite propaganda. All that will remain for Czechoslovakia is to come to terms
> 5 with Germany. Austria does not conceal her anxiety. 'Next time it will be our turn' ... Turkey, who has increasingly close economic relations with Germany, but who politically remains in the Franco-British axis can be induced to modify her line. The Scandinavian countries ... are alarmed.

# 7 The Spanish Civil War

> **KEY ISSUE** How did the great powers react to the Spanish Civil War?

The civil war in Spain was essentially a domestic matter which rapidly became an international issue threatening to involve the major powers in a European conflict. It began in July 1936 with a Nationalist revolt led by the army against the Spanish Republican government. When the rebels were defeated in a number of cities by armed workers' militias, both sides appealed to the international community for help. The Nationalists, led by General Franco, looked to Germany and Italy, while the Republicans approached Britain, France and Soviet Russia. In 1946 at the Nuremberg trials Göring, had been the commander of the German Air Force in 1936, recalled Franco's request:

> 1 When the Civil War broke out in Spain ... Franco sent a call for help to Germany and asked for support, particularly in the air. Franco with his troops was stationed in Africa and ... could not get his troops across, as the fleet was in the hands of the Communists ... The decisive factor
> 5 was, first of all, to get his troops to Spain ... The Führer thought the

matter over. I urged him to give support under all circumstances; firstly to prevent the further spread of Communism; secondly, to test my young *Luftwaffe* [air force] in this or that technical aspect.

Hitler quickly agreed to provide a fleet of transport aircraft to fly Franco's men across to Spain. He then followed this up with the dispatch of some 6000 troops. Hitler's motives for providing assistance were probably more complex than Göring indicated. Hitler later claimed that he wanted to distract the western powers so that he could continue to rearm without fear of intervention. He was also aware of the advantages of having a friendly government in Madrid which would not only supply Germany with Spanish mineral resources but would also in wartime possibly provide bases for German submarines. Mussolini, also after some hesitation, as he wanted to keep open the option of resurrecting the Stresa Front, agreed to assist Franco for the same mixture of ideological and strategic reasons: he hoped to defeat the Left in Spain, gain a new ally in Franco and 'strengthen' the Italian character by exposure to war.

With both Germany and Italy openly helping Franco there was a real danger of a European war, should France and Britain be drawn in on the Republican side. When the French Prime Minister, Léon Blum, se power rested on a left-wing coalition, was first asked for help by the Republic, he was tempted to send it, if only to deny potential allies of Germany a victory in Spain. However, two factors forced him to have second thoughts. Firstly the actual dispatch of French military aid to the Republicans would have polarised French society, which was already deeply divided between Right and Left, and run the risk of plunging France into a civil war of its own; and secondly the British government came out strongly against intervention. The British Ambassador in Paris even threatened neutrality should French assistance to the Republicans lead to war with Germany. Despite the strategic dangers for Britain's position in the Mediterranean in the event of a Nationalist victory, the Cabinet viewed the civil war as essentially a side-issue which must not be allowed to prevent its continued search for a lasting settlement with Germany. In addition, there were powerful voices within the Conservative Party  actively sympathised with Franco.

The Republican government therefore had little option but to approach Soviet Russia for help. In September 1936 Stalin sent hundreds of military advisers and large quantities of military equipment, while the Comintern (the Communist International organisation based in Moscow) was made responsible for recruiting brigades of international volunteers. Stalin, like Hitler, saw the civil war as a way of dividing his enemies. In a bitter attack on the non-intervention policies of Britain and France, Stalin in fact described one of the aims of his own policy:

1 There shines through the policy of non intervention the desire ... to permit all the participants ... to become deeply bogged down in the

mire of the war, to encourage them surreptitiously in this direction, to
let them weaken and exhaust each other ... and then when they are suf-
5 ficiently weakened, to come on to the scene with fresh forces ... and to
dictate one's terms to the weakened participants in the war.

A conflict between the Western Powers and Germany would certainly
have suited Stalin's policy, but he was also anxious to prevent a
Nationalist victory in Spain since this would strengthen the forces of
international Fascism and make a German attack on the Soviet Union
more likely.

In an attempt to prevent the war spreading, Britain and France
proposed a non-intervention agreement. This was signed by the other
European powers, but Germany and Italy ignored it and continued to
assist Franco. Stalin likewise went on helping the Republicans, but by
early 1937, when he realised that they could not win, he reduced the
flow of arms to a level that was just sufficient to prolong the conflict.
In this he was successful, as it was not until March 1939 that Franco at
last occupied Madrid.

For the Democracies the civil war could not have come at a worse
time. It polarised public opinion between Right and Left, threatened
France with encirclement and cemented the Italian–German rap-
prochement. It may also have helped to convince the Soviet Union of
the weakness of the West and prepared the way for the Nazi–Soviet
Pact of September 1939 (see pages 135–7). As with the Abyssinian
crisis, it was undoubtedly Germany which benefited most from the
conflict since it diverted the attention of the powers during the crucial period 1936–7 from the Nazi rearmament programme.

# 8 The Rome–Berlin Axis and the Anti-Comintern Pact

> **KEY ISSUES** Why and how did Japan, Germany and Italy draw
> closer to together in the period 1936–7?

The summer of 1936 saw increasingly cordial relations between Berlin
and Rome. While Britain pointedly refused to recognise the King of
Italy as the 'Emperor of Abyssinia', Germany rapidly did so. Hitler
and Mussolini also cooperated in blocking a new British initiative to
up-date the Locarno Treaty. Italy's growing hostility towards Britain,
France and especially Russia, with m until the Spanish Civil War it had
enjoyed good relations, also ensured the need to be more
tolerant of German influence in Austria. In January 1936 Mussolini
assured the German Ambassador in Rome that

> If Austria, as a formerly independent state, were ... in practice to
> become a German satellite, he would have no objection.

On 11 July an Austro-German agreement was successfully negotiated on this basis. Germany recognised Austrian independence, while Vienna promised to pursue a German-orientated foreign policy and to bring leading Nazis into government. This removed the most contentious issue between Italy and Germany and prepared the way for a German–Italian agreement, the October Protocols, which were signed in Berlin in October 1936. Mussolini announced this new alignment to the world at a mass meeting in Milan on 1 November:

1  The Berlin conversations have resulted in an understanding between
   our two countries over certain problems which have been particularly
   acute. By these understandings ... this Berlin-Rome line is ... an axis
   around which can revolve all those European states with a will to col-
5  laboration and peace.

Three weeks later Hitler overrode advice from his professional diplomats and signed the Anti-Comintern Pact with Japan. This was more of symbolic than practical importance as it was aimed against the Communist International (Comintern) rather than the Soviet Union itself. Its value for Japan was that, at a time when it was facing increasing hostility from China and Russia in the Far East, it could signal to Moscow that it was no longer isolated. For Hitler, too, coming so soon after the Rome–Berlin Axis, it showed the world that Germany was no longer alone, as it had appeared to be in the spring of 1935. In November 1937 the Pact was further strengthened by Italy's accession.

# 9 Assessment

> **KEY ISSUE** In what ways, and for what reasons, had the situation in Europe been transformed from 1930 to 1937?

Between 1930 and 1937 there was what amounted to a 'diplomatic revolution' in international affairs. Germany and Japan had left the League to be followed by Italy in December 1937, key clauses of the Versailles Treaty had been broken and the Locarno Agreements had been shown to be worthless when Nazi Germany remilitarised the Rhineland. In 1930 Britain and France, thanks to their victories in the war, had still dominated Europe. Although the German economy had staged a partial recovery, Berlin was committed to cooperation with Britain and France and was in many ways still dependent on them. Both the USSR and Italy remained marginal powers. By 1937 all this had changed. Germany had begun to rearm and by re-occupying the Rhineland had made it virtually impossible for the Western powers to threaten Berlin with military sanctions again. Japan had broken free from American domination in the Far East and Italy had defied the

League to occupy Abyssinia. Britain, France and even the USA would now have to come to terms with the fact that 'a new globe spanning alliance',[12] as Gerhard Weinberg has described it, was apparently being created which could threaten them simultaneously on both sides of the world. It was now the Democracies and not Germany that were on the defensive.

## References

1  R. Boyce, 'World Depression, World War: Some Economic Origins of the Second World War' in R. Boyce and E.M. Robertson (eds), *Paths to War: New Essays on the Origins of the Second World War* (Basingstoke, Macmillan, 1989), p. 55.
2  Quoted in M. Lamb and N. Tarling, *From Versailles to Pearl Harbor* (Basingstoke, Palgrave, 2001), p. 88.
3  Ibid., p. 90.
4  J. Hiden, *Germany and Europe, 1919–1939* (London, Longman, 1977), p. 63.
5  P. Krüger, *Die Aussenpolitik der Republik von Weimar* (Darmstadt, Wissenschaftliche Buchgesellschaft, 1985), p. 529.
6  Northedge, *The League of Nations: Its Life and Times* (Leicester University Press, 1988), p. 127.
7  A.J.P. Taylor, *The Origins of the Second World War* (London, Routledge, 1961), p. 68.
8  H. Mommsen, 'National Socialism: Continuity and Change' in W. Laqueur (ed.), *Fascism* (Harmondsworth, Penguin, 1979), p. 177.
9  For the Programme School arguments, see K. Hildebrand, *The Foreign Policy of the Third Reich* (London, Batsford, 1973).
10  A. Bullock, 'Hitler and the Origins of the Second World War' in E. Robertson (ed.), *The Origins of the Second World War* (London, Macmillan, 1971), p. 193.
11  Quoted in A. Adamthwaite, *The Making of the Second World War* (London, Allen and Unwin, 1977), p. 44.
12  G. Weinberg, *The Foreign Policy of Hitler's Germany* (Chicago, University of Chicago Press, 1983), p. 348.

## Summary Diagram
The Rise of Nazi Germany

| Attempts to contain Nazi Germany, 1933–7 | | | |
|---|---|---|---|
| Franco-Soviet Pact May 1935 | The Stresa Declaration April 1935 | Franco-Italian Rome Agreements January 1935 | League Disarmament Conference 1932–4 |

| Nazi Germany seizes the initiative | | | | | | |
|---|---|---|---|---|---|---|
| Quits League of Nations October 1933 | German-Polish Agreement January 1934 | Anglo-German Naval Agreement June 1935 | Exploits Abyssinian Crisis | Exploits Spanish Civil War | Signs Axis Agreement October 1936 | Anti-Comintern Pact November 1936 |

| Reaction of the great powers to Spanish Cvil War | | | | |
|---|---|---|---|---|
| **Germany** | **Italy** | **USSR** | **Britain** | **France** |
| Sends troops Hopes to keep war going to distract Britain and France | Wants Franco as an ally against Britain and France | Assists Republicans | Proposes non-intervention | Backs Britsh proposals |

## Working on Chapter 5

As you re-read this chapter and make notes on it, first of all try to identify why and how the Great Depression helped to weaken the peace settlements and bring to power politicians, who were increasingly ready to act unilaterally to defend their countries' interests. You will need to look carefully at the significance of the Manchurian incident and then at the rise of Hitler and at his foreign policy. Ask yourself whether this policy had any continuities with Brüning's or even Stresemann's policies, or was it just that up to 1936 he had to be cautious and lead the great powers into believing that, like all Germans, he wished to revise peacefully the Treaty of Versailles, rather than wage a war of conquest. It is also important to note carefully the ambiguous reaction of the European powers to Nazi Germany. On the one hand, they did start to draw nearer as the Stresa Front and the Franco-Soviet treaty showed; yet each power also attempted to negotiate with Hitler directly. A key issue in this chapter is also how, through the Axis Agreement and the Anti-Comintern Pact, Nazi Germany, Italy and Japan began to draw together. Ask yourself how this was possible, given that Italy played a key role in building up the Stresa Front in 1935. To answer this you will need to look carefully the impact of the Abyssinian and Spanish Civil Wars on the situation in Europe.

## Answering structured and essay questions on Chapter 5

The years 1930–7 are an important watershed in the interwar years, as they see the collapse of the League and the Locarno system and the emergence of Nazi Germany. You ought therefore to be ready to answer detailed questions on this period. Consider the following structured questions:

1  **a)**  Outline briefly the Manchurian crisis of 1931–2.
   **b)**  Explain the consequences of this crisis.
2  **a)**  Outline the progress Hitler had made in destroying the Treaty of Versailles by the end of 1936.
   **b)**  Why was he so successful?
3  **a)**  Outline briefly how Japan, Italy and Germany had moved closer to each other by the end of 1937.
   **b)**  What was the impact of the Abyssinian war on international politics?

The examiner requires you to 'recall, select and deploy knowledge accurately, and communicate knowledge and understanding of history in a clear and effective manner'. Part a) of these questions tests your ability to do this concisely. Part b) tests you on the more difficult skills of 'understanding, explaining and assessing'. Thus in 2b), for instance, you would gain very few marks if you just recapitulated what you had stated in 2a). The crucial question you have to answer is *why* he was successful, and therefore you must consider the importance of such factors as the Depression, the lack of unity amongst the other European powers and the impact of the Abyssinian war.

Here are some examples of essay questions. Study the following questions which are a mixture of detailed and more general topics:

1  What were the international consequences of the Great Depression?
2  Account for the collapse of the Versailles and Locarno systems by 1936.
3  Why were the great powers so ineffective in containing Hitler, 1933–6?
4  To what extent did Hitler merely follow the policy of his predecessors up to the end of 1936?
5  Compare and contrast the damage done to the League of Nations by the Manchurian and Abyssinian crises.

The basic themes underlying questions on the period 1930–6 are the impact of the Great Depression on international relations and the collapse of collective security. The destructive consequences of the Depression are explored most directly in the first three questions.

Question 1 is the most straightforward, but in answering it you must be careful not to give just an account of events in Manchuria, of Brüning's and Hitler's foreign policy, America's retreat into isolation, etc. You must show *how* and *why* the Depression acted as a catalyst for many of these events. Before writing the essay it would be a good idea to draw up a list of the major consequences in order of importance. Questions 2 and 3 are more complicated in that they focus more indirectly on the Depression. In Question 2 was it the Depression which brought about the eventual collapse of the Versailles and Locarno systems by bringing Hitler to power? Or were there other factors, such as the traditional reluctance of Britain and America to guarantee French security, which operated quite independently of the Depression? Question 3 similarly requires you to assess how a combination of factors made the efforts of the great powers to contain Germany ineffectual. It would be useful to make a plan of the different points – backed by evidence- which you could use here. Of course the Depression would figure, but is this the whole story? How would you, for instance, evaluate Hitler's own successful attempts to avoid openly challenging the powers until 1936? Why did Britain and France so mishandle the Abyssinian crisis? Why was the outbreak of the Spanish Civil War good news for Hitler? Question 4 focuses on the question of the continuity of German foreign policy. To answer this you will need to re-read your notes on Stresemann from Chapter 4. Then draw up a list of the similarities and differences between the foreign policy of Hitler and his predecessors. It will be particularly important to explore not only their short-term policies but also their ultimate aims. How would you go on to plan Question 5? Remember that the surest way of writing a poor answer would be just to 'tell the story' first of the Manchurian crisis and then of the Abyssinian crisis. You need to treat the two crises thematically and to keep making contrasts and comparisons right through your essay.

## Source-based questions on Chapter 5

1 **German Foreign Policy, 1930–6**
Carefully read the extracts from *Mein Kampf* on page 100 (Source A), Bülow's memorandum on pages 101–2 (Source B) and Hitler's speech on page 102 (Source C). Answer the following questions.
   **a)** Study Source A.
   What was the new foreign policy that Hitler was proposing in 1924? (*3 marks*)
   **b)** Study Source B and use your own knowledge.
   Why is Bülow advising Hitler to proceed carefully in 1934? (*5 marks*)
   **c)** Study all the sources and use your own knowledge.
   Do you agree with the view that Hitler was in reality a cautious politician and that his aim to expand eastwards was just a dream?

**2** **The Reactions of Britain, France and Russia to Nazi Germany**
Read carefully the comments by Paul-Boncour (Source A) and the French
Ambassador (Source B) on page 104, the summary by Sir John Simon
(Source C) and the suggestions in the Cabinet on (Source D) pages 105–6
and Stalin's speech on page 107 (Source E). Answer the following questions:
**a)** Study Sources A and B.
How far does source A support the argument put forward in Source
B about the need for a Franco-Russian alliance? (*5 marks*)
**b)** Study Sources C, D and E.
Compare the values of these sources as evidence for the historian
enquiring into the reaction of Britain and Russia to the rise of Hitler.
(*5 marks*)
**c)** Study all the sources and use your own knowledge.
Do you agree with the view that Nazi expansionism could easily have
been stopped in the period 1933–5?

**3** **The Manchurian and Abyssinian Crises**
Carefully read the extracts from the Lytton Commission on page 98
(Source A), Sir John Simon's speech on page 98 (Source B), Sir Robert
Vansittart's statement on page 109 (Source C), Hugh Dalton's speech on
page 112 (Source D) and the French memorandum of 12 March 1936 on
page 112 (Source E). Also look at the cartoon on page 110 (Source F).
Answer the following questions:
**a)** Study Source A.
What does Sir John Simon mean when he calls himself 'enough of a
pacifist' (line 1)? (*2 marks*)
**b)** Study Sources C and F.
How far does the message of Source F support the argument put forward in source C about the need to find a compromise with Italy over
Abyssinia? (*6 marks*)
**c)** Study all the Sources and use your own knowledge.
Do you agree with the view the that Britain and France gravely mis-
handled both the Manchurian and the Abyssinian crises with disastrous
consequences. (*12 marks*)

**4** **The Spanish Civil War**
Carefully read the statements by Göring on pages 112–13 (Source A) and
Stalin on page 113–14 (Source B). Answer the following questions:
**a)** Study Source B and use your own knowledge.
Briefly explain the meaning of 'non-intervention' (line 1). (*3 marks*)
**b)** Study Source A.
What can you learn from Source A about the reasons for German
intervention in Spain? (*7 marks*)
**c)** Study Sources A and B.
How far do these two sources support the view that that neither Stalin
nor Hitler wanted a quick peace in Spain? Explain your answer fully.
(*10 marks*)

# 6 The Countdown to War

## POINTS TO CONSIDER

This chapter focuses first of all on the outbreak of the Sino-Japanese war, which put pressure on the British and French Far Eastern Empires and made the USA more determined to avoid war in Europe. It then considers Hitler's plans for expansion and looks at how this expansion actually occurred in Central Europe. The core of this chapter covers the crucial period from March 1938 to September 1939 when Germany annexed Austria, was given the Sudetenland at the Munich Conference and then went on to dismember Czechoslovakia. It ends with Hitler's attack on Poland, which triggered the Second World War. As you read through the chapter, ask yourself why the Anglo-French policy of appeasement failed, and why Britain suddenly did a 'u-turn' and guaranteed Poland in March 1939. Consider whether Neville Chamberlain, the British Prime Minister, could have prevented war by adopting a policy of deterrence against Germany at an earlier date. It is also important to ask yourself why Stalin did an about-turn in the opposite direction and moved from opposing Hitler to signing the Nazi–Soviet Pact.

## KEY DATES

| | | |
|---|---|---|
| **1937** | July | Japan attacked China |
| **1938** | 12 March | German occupation of Austria |
| | 20–2 May | Rumours that Germany was about to invade Czechoslovakia |
| | 8 September | Sudeten Germans broke off negotiations with Prague |
| | 15 September | Chamberlain visited Hitler at Berchtesgaden |
| | 22–3 September | Chamberlain at Bad Godesberg |
| | 28 September | Hitler accepted Mussolini's plan for Four-Power talks |
| | 29–30 September | Four-Power Conference at Munich |
| **1939** | 15 March | Germany occupied Bohemia and Moravia |
| | 21 March | German–Polish talks on Danzig |
| | 23 March | Lithuania handed over Memel to Germany |
| | 31 March | Provisional Anglo-French guarantee of Poland |
| | 7 April | Italian occupation of Albania |
| | 13 April | Anglo-French guarantee of Greece and Romania |
| | 14 April | Anglo-French negotiations with Soviet Union start |
| | 28 April | Hitler terminated Anglo-German Naval Agreement and German–Polish Pact |

22 May            Pact of Steel signed in Berlin
23 August         Nazi–Soviet Pact
1 September        Germany invaded Poland
3 September        Britain and France declared war on Germany

# 1 The Outbreak of the Sino-Japanese War

> **KEY ISSUES** What were Japanese aims in China? What impact did the war have on Britain, France and the USA?

The war in the Far East which ended with the dropping of atom bombs on Hiroshima and Nagasaki in 1945 began when a minor incident involving Japanese and Nationalist Chinese troops at the Marco-Polo bridge near Beijing on 7 July 1937 and then rapidly escalated into full-scale hostilities. Japan was determined to turn northern China into an economic and political satellite and progressively to extend its influence throughout the whole of south-east Asia at the cost of America and the European colonial empires.

Inevitably the war emphasised the fragility of British and French power as neither country could afford simultaneous hostilities in Europe and the Far East. Thus, as tension mounted in Europe, both governments in practice avoided confrontation with the Japanese. In 1937 a senior French diplomat bluntly informed the American ambassador in Paris that:

1   ... as long as the present tension existed in Europe it would be impossible for France to take part in any common action in the Far East, which might imply at some stage the furnishing [provision] of armed forces ...
    It was regrettable that this situation existed ... but the situation was a
5   fact and had to be faced.

Although America was equally reluctant to take military measures against Japan, the spreading conflict did enable President Roosevelt to begin the slow process of re-aligning America with the democracies against the Axis powers and Japan. In September 1937, in his famous 'Quarantine Speech', he warned the American people that:

> War is a contagion whether it be declared or undeclared. It can engulf states and peoples remote from the original scene of hostilities. We are determined to keep out of war, yet we cannot insure ourselves against the disastrous effects of war and the dangers of involvement.

In December 1937, when British and American ships on the Yangtzee river were attacked by Japanese planes, Roosevelt, despite immediate Japanese apologies and offers of compensation, took the potentially important step of sending an American naval officer to discuss possible future cooperation between the British and American fleets; but when Congress found out, there was an explosion of anger and Roosevelt was severely criticised for compromising American neutrality. No wonder that Neville Chamberlain observed that 'It is always best and safest to count on nothing from the Americans but words'.[1]

While the Far Eastern War increased the pressure on Britain and France, it did not automatically follow that Japan, Italy and Germany would find it easy to form a common front against the democracies. The Germans had built up a profitable arms trade with China, and they also feared that Japan might become bogged down in a long war against the Chinese and so in practice become less of a threat to the West. On the other hand, in July 1937 Japan was anxious for diplomatic support from Italy and Germany but did not want to run the risk of becoming involved in a premature war against Britain and France as a result of a European quarrel. The solution proposed by Berlin, that Italy should join Japan and Germany in the Anti-Comintern Pact in November 1937, was a clever compromise. It associated Japan with the two Axis powers in a vague and symbolic pact that was primarily anti-Communist (see page 115), but which potentially could also be directed against the Western powers as well. Significantly, in the summer of 1939 Japan refused to agree to the Pact's conversion into a military alliance, as at a time of mounting tension with Russia, it wished to avoid war with Britain and France. Nevertheless, the Pact had considerable political value for Japan. By associating itself with the Axis powers, it could avoid isolation and play on Franco-British fears of a simultaneous conflict in Europe and the Far East to extract further concessions from them.

## 2 Hitler Considers his Options

> **KEY ISSUE** How seriously should historians take the 'Hossbach Memorandum'?

By the autumn of 1937 Hitler had dismantled the Locarno and Versailles systems. The Spanish Civil War and the Sino-Japanese War distracted his potential enemies, while Italy was drawing ever closer to Berlin. In August 1936 he had initiated the 'Four Year Plan' for preparing the German economy for war by 1940. He was thus in a favourable position to consider options for a new and more aggressive phase of foreign policy. Some historians like T. Mason[2] argue that Hitler in reality had no alternative but to go to war. His over-rapid rearmament programme, which was to a great extent dependent on foreign imports, was threatening to plunge the German economy into a major crisis. Only the seizure of new supplies of raw materials, foodstuffs and gold reserves could avert economic collapse. The economy probably was in danger of overheating, but, as W. Carr[3] has pointed out, it is by no means easy to establish that Hitler went to war merely to avoid a developing economic crisis.

On 5 November 1937 Hitler called a special meeting which was attended by his Commanders-in-Chief and Foreign and War Ministers. Hitler told them that what he had to say was so important that it was to be regarded as 'his last will and testament'. He then continued:

1  The aim of German policy was to make secure and to preserve the racial community and to enlarge it. It was therefore a question of space ... [Lebensraum] The question for Germany was: Where could she achieve the greatest gain at the lowest cost? German policy had to
5  reckon with two hate inspired antagonists, Britain and France, to whom a German colossus in the centre of Europe was a thorn in the flesh ... Germany's problem could only be solved by the use of force ... If the resort to force with its attendant risks is accepted ... there then remains still to be answered the questions 'When'? and 'How'? In this
10  matter there were three contingencies to be dealt with.

Contingency 1: Period 1943–5

After that date only a change for the worse, from our point of view, could be expected ... Our relative strength would decrease in relation
15  to the rearmament which would then have been carried out by the rest of the world. If we did not act by 1943–5 any year could, owing to lack of reserves, produce the food crisis ... and this must be regarded as a 'waning point of the regime' ... If the Führer was still living, it was his unalterable determination to solve Germany's problem of space by
20  1943–5 at the latest ...

Contingency 2

If internal strife in France should develop into such a domestic crisis as to absorb the French army completely and render it incapable of use
25  for war against Germany, then the time for acting against the Czechs would have come.

Contingency 3

If France should be so embroiled in war with another state that she
30  could not 'proceed' against Germany. For the improvement of our politico-military position our first objective, in the event of our being embroiled in war, must be to overthrow Czechoslovakia and Austria simultaneously in order to remove the threat to our flank in any possible operation against the West ...

In a brilliant analysis A.J.P. Taylor has shown that this document, which was compiled by Hitler's adjutant (military assistant), Colonel Hossbach, some 5 days after the meeting, is in fact a fragment of a copy of the original that has disappeared. Moreover, the meeting it records was in fact not primarily concerned with the aims of foreign policy but with the allocation of armaments between the German armed services. The document has therefore lost some of the significance which was attributed to it when it was used by the prosecution at the Nuremberg War Crimes Trials in 1946. However, few historians agree with Taylor's conclusions that Hitler's exposition was for the most part 'day dreaming unrelated to what followed in real life' and that he was in fact 'at a loss what to do next even after he had the power to do it'.[4] The consensus of research still decisively favours W. Carr's view that Hitler was warning his generals 'that a more adventurous and dangerous foreign policy was imminent'.[5] As you read this chapter you must make up your own mind about the significance of the 'Hossbach Memorandum'.

# 3 Britain, France and Appeasement

> **KEY ISSUES** What are the historical arguments about appeasement and why and how did Chamberlain launch a policy of appeasement in the autumn of 1937?

In the first 20 years after the defeat of Hitler historians on both the Right and Left scornfully dismissed appeasement. They were heavily influenced not only by Winston Churchill's memoirs, but also by a brilliant pamphlet, *Guilty Men*,[6] which was written by three left-wing journalists, including Michael Foot, later a leader of the Labour Party. It was published in July 1940, just a few weeks after the fall of France and the evacuation from Dunkirk, and bitterly accused Chamberlain of pursuing a disastrous policy which left Britain unprepared militarily to face the dictators. In the eyes of the general public and historians, Neville Chamberlain, who became Prime Minister in May 1937, rapidly became the scapegoat for these events. French historians and politicians claimed also that he had bullied them into appeasement, while some Germans were tempted to excuse their own support for Hitler by blaming Chamberlain for not standing up to the Nazis.

## APPEASEMENT

Appeasement had been a traditional British policy since, at the very least, the early 1900s. It was in many ways a realistic policy based on the need to compromise by a large and vulnerable empire. Austen Chamberlain (see Chapter 4) had frequently talked about the need to appease Germany in the 1920s. Concessions to Stresemann's Germany did indeed work, but making concessions to Nazi Germany clearly did not!

Only with the opening up of the British and French archives in the 1960s and 1970s did it gradually become possible to reassess the whole policy of appeasement. Now historians like K. Robbins and K. Middlemas[7] were able to place Chamberlain's policy of appeasement in the context of Britain's slow economic decline as well as the global challenges facing the British Empire. R. P. Shay[8] in his study of British rearmament in the 1930s argues that Chamberlain had to maintain a balance between rearming and balancing the budget, so that if war came, Britain would have enough money to buy vital materials and equipment from the USA. By the end of the 1980s revisionist historians were arguing that Chamberlain's policy was essentially determined by Britain's weakness and that he had no other option but to attempt to appease Germany, if the Empire was to be preserved. John Charmley[9] even argued that Churchill was the real 'Guilty man' by fighting a war that could only end in the dissolution of the Empire and bankruptcy. This revisionist line was, however, strongly challenged by R.A.C. Parker both in his book *Chamberlain and Appeasement* and then in his later study, *Churchill and Appeasement*,[10] in which he argued that this interpretation was too deterministic and ignored any possibility that Chamberlain could have pursued a different policy. Parker insists in the former book that

> After the *Anschluss* [see below] in March 1938 Chamberlain could ... have secured sufficient support in Britain for a close alliance with France, and a policy of containing and encircling Germany, more or less shrouded under the League of Nations covenant.

France was in a similar position to Britain. It, too, was threatened in the Mediterranean by Italy and in the Far East by Japan. Its economy, however, was much weaker than Britain's. Between 1936 and 1938 the franc had to be devalued three times to help pay for rearmament. By 1937 France was dependent on Britain not only economically but also politically. French society was deeply divided as the Right wanted to negotiate with Hitler and Mussolini, while the Left wanted to fight and looked to Russia as an ally. It has been argued that only by allowing Britain to take the lead in negotiating with Germany, and therefore the blame for difficult decisions and possible failures, could French politicians preserve the semblance of social unity in their country. It is not surprising therefore that it was left to Chamberlain, who became Prime Minister in May 1937, to give appeasement its real momentum.

Chamberlain aimed first to repair Anglo-Italian relations with the intention of encouraging Mussolini to restrain Hitler, but opposition from his Foreign Secretary, Anthony Eden, delayed talks until February 1938. In April a preliminary agreement was reached to respect the status quo in the Mediterranean, but it was never implemented because Mussolini did not punctually withdraw his troops from Spain as he had promised to do. Nevertheless, as we shall see, Mussolini did play a crucial moderating role during the Sudeten crisis in September

1938 and he did remain neutral when war broke out in September 1939. Arguably, however, this was not so much a consequence of Chamberlain's diplomacy but rather of Italy's military and economic weakness.

In the autumn of 1937 Chamberlain launched a major initiative aimed at achieving a settlement with Hitler. Initially, at any rate, appeasement, was a hard-headed attempt to slow up the pace of German expansion in eastern Europe by offering Germany colonies in Africa, while giving both Britain and France time to accelerate their rearmament programmes. In late November an Anglo-French summit was held in London where this policy was more fully explored. Chamberlain argued:

> 1  It seemed desirable to try to achieve some agreement with Germany on Central Europe whatever might be Germany's aims. Even if she wished to absorb some of her neighbours; one could in effect hope to delay the execution of German plans, and even to restrain the Reich for
> 5  such a time that its plans might become impractical in the long run.

Chamberlain won over the French to this policy and by March 1938 he was ready to negotiate a package of colonial concessions with Berlin, but the gathering pace of German expansion signalled first by the *Anschluss* and then by the destruction of Czechoslovakia made this approach irrelevant.

# 4  The *Anschluss* and the Destruction of Czechoslovakia

> **KEY ISSUES**  How was Hitler able to annex Austria and the Sudetenland and destroy Czechoslovakia? What were the reactions of Britain and France to these events?

In November 1937 Hitler had outlined a possible scenario involving civil war in France or a Franco-Italian war (see page 124), which would enable him to annex Austria and dismember Czechoslovakia without fear of international intervention. He was able to achieve these aims in 1938–9, even though the circumstances, which he had predicted, never in fact came about. Both the *Anschluss*, and the eventual destruction of Czechoslovakia do indeed show Hitler's ability to adapt his tactics to the prevailing circumstances whilst steadily pursuing his overall aims.

## a) The Anschluss

The annexation of Austria had long been a key aim of Nazi foreign policy, but Hitler did not plan the actual events that enabled him to achieve it. The crisis was ultimately triggered when Schuschnigg, the Austrian Chancellor, alarmed by the activities of the Austrian Nazis, requested an interview with Hitler. Hitler welcomed the chance to achieve an easy diplomatic success by imposing on Schuschnigg an agreement which would not only have subordinated Austrian foreign policy to Berlin but also have given the Austrian Nazi Party complete freedom. However, Schuschnigg then decided unexpectedly to regain some room for manoeuvre by asking his countrymen to vote in a referendum, which he planned to hold on Sunday 14 March, for a 'free and German, independent and social, Christian and united Austria'.

The immediate danger for the German government was that if Schuschnigg's appeal was endorsed by a large majority, he would be able to renounce his agreement with Hitler. Confronted by this challenge, Hitler rapidly dropped his policy of gradual absorption of Austria and not only forced Schuschnigg to cancel the referendum but on 12 March ordered the German army to occupy Austria. Then Hitler decided, apparently on the spur of the moment after a highly successful visit to the Austrian city of Linz where he had attended secondary school as a boy, to incorporate Austria into the Reich rather than install a satellite Nazi government in Vienna.

Besides violating the Treaty of Versailles, which specifically forbade the union of Germany and Austria (see page 36), Hitler had for the first time invaded an independent state, even though the Austrian army did not oppose him, and put himself in a position from which to threaten Czechoslovakia. Why then did this not bring about a repetition of the Stresa Front that was briefly formed in 1935 against German aggression (see page 102)? Although Chamberlain was in contact with the Italian government, and in April concluded an agreement aimed at lowering the tension in the Mediterranean, Mussolini had decided as long ago as 1936 that Austria was a German sphere of interest. Not surprisingly therefore, on 11 March, he backed Hitler's decision to invade Austria. Both Britain and France protested to Berlin but neither had any intention of going to war over Austria. Indeed the French were paralysed by an internal political crisis caused by the resignation of the Chautemps ministry. and between 10 and 13 March did not even have a government.

The initial reaction of the British government was to hope that the storm would blow over and that talks could resume with Berlin on a package of possible colonial concessions (see page 127), which had already been handed to the German government on 3 March. These concessions were, after all, aimed to distract Berlin from pursuing its ambitions in central Europe. Whether Chamberlain really believed that Hitler could be bought off is hard to say. Privately he wrote that in March 1938 'it was now clear' that force was the only argument that Germany understood',[11] but publicly he was not yet ready to draw the logical conclusion from this and confront Hitler. Was he gaining time

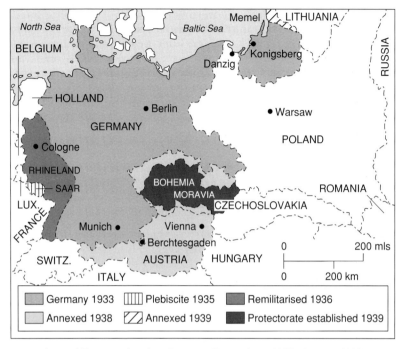

Central Europe showing German Expansion, 1935–August 1939.

for his country to re-arm or was he seriously giving peace one more chance?

## b) The Sudeten Crisis

The annexation of Austria with the minimum of international protest greatly increased the vulnerability of Czechoslovakia to Nazi pressure, as it was now surrounded on three sides by German territory. Hitler had long regarded Czechoslovakia, with its alliances with both France and Russia, as a strategic threat to Germany which would eventually have to be eliminated. It is, however, arguable that in April 1938 Hitler was by no means sure how he was to carry out this aim. He certainly played with the idea of launching a sudden attack on Czechoslovakia if a major crisis were to be triggered, for instance by the assassination of the German ambassador in Prague. An easier and safer way to bring about the disintegration of Czechoslovakia was to inflame the nationalism of the Sudeten Germans. Czechoslovakia was a fragile state undermined by an ethnically divided population. Its unity was particularly threatened by the 3 million Sudeten Germans and the 2 million Slovaks. Hitler therefore specifically instructed Konrad Henlein, the Sudeten German leader, to keep making demands for concessions which the Prague government could not possibly grant if it wanted to preserve the unity of Czechoslovakia.

In the aftermath of the *Anschluss* both Britain and France were acutely aware of the growing threat to Czechoslovakia. Britain was unwilling to guarantee Czechoslovakia and yet realised that it might well not be able to stand aloof from the consequences of a German attack upon it. Chamberlain told the Commons on 24 March that if fighting occurred:

1   it would be well within the bounds of possibility that other countries, besides those which were parties to the original dispute, would almost immediately become involved. This is especially true in the case of two countries like Great Britain and France, with long associations of friend-
5   ship, with interests closely interwoven, devoted to the same ideals of democratic liberty and determined to uphold them.

The French, unlike the British, were pledged by two treaties signed in 1924 and 1925 to consult and assist Czechoslovakia in the event of a threat to their common interests. In reality the French were in no position to help the Czechs. The Chief of the French Air Staff made no secret of his fears that the French air force would be wiped out within 15 days after the outbreak of war with Germany. The French Government was therefore ready to follow the British lead in seeking a way of defusing the Sudeten crisis before it could lead to war.

The urgency of this was underlined by the war scare of the week-end of 20–1 May, when the Czech government suddenly partially mobilised its army in response to false rumours that a German attack was imminent. Hitler, warned by both Britain and France of the dangerous consequences of any military action, rapidly proclaimed the absence of any mobilisation plans. Yet far from making Hitler more reasonable, this incident appears to have had the opposite effect, as he immediately stepped up military preparations for an invasion and set 1 October as a deadline for 'smashing Czechoslovakia'. Taylor sees this as bluff and argues that 'Hitler did not need to act. Others would do his work for him'.[12] There were certainly, as we have seen, powerful forces working for the disintegration of the Czech state, but most historians do not dismiss Hitler's plans so lightly. It is more likely that he was just keeping his options open, as Bullock argues, to the very last possible moment'.[13]

Meanwhile, France and Britain were redoubling their efforts to find a peaceful solution. The Anglo-French peace strategy aimed to put pressure on both the Czechs and the Sudeten Germans to make concessions, while continuing to warn Hitler of the dangers of a general war. In early September Benes, the Czech Prime Minister, responded to this pressure by granting almost all Henlein's demands. As this threatened the justification for Hitler's campaign against Czechoslovakia, Hitler immediately instructed Henlein to provoke a

Armed Sudeten volunteers preparing to assist a German invasion

series of incidents which would enable him to break off negotiations with Benes.

On 12 September 1938 Hitler's campaign moved into a new phase when, in a speech at the Nuremberg rally, he violently attacked the Czechs and assured the Sudetens of his support. Both Britain and France desperately attempted to avoid war. Daladier, the French Prime Minister, suggested that he and Chamberlain should meet Hitler, but Chamberlain seized the initiative and flew alone to see Hitler on 15 September at Berchtesgaden. There he agreed, subject to consultation with the French, that Czechoslovakia should cede to Germany all areas which contained a German population of 50% or over. This would be supervised by an international commission. Hitler also demanded that Czechoslovakia should renounce its pact with Soviet Russia. When Chamberlain again met Hitler at Bad Godesberg on 22 September, after winning French backing for his plan, Hitler demanded that the German occupation of the Sudetenland should be speeded up so that it would be completed by 28 September. Nor was it to be supervised by any international commission. Why Hitler should suddenly have changed his mind has puzzled historians. Taylor argued that Hitler was anxious to avoid accepting Chamberlain's plan in the hope that the Hungarians and Poles would formulate their own demands for Czechoslovakian territory and that he would then be able to move in and occupy the whole state under the pretext of being 'a peace-maker creating a 'new order'.[14] On the other hand it is possible that Hitler had no such elaborate plan in mind and merely wanted to eliminate Czechoslovakia once and for all through war. At this stage Chamberlain's peace initiative seemed to have failed. France and Britain reluctantly began to mobilise, although both powers still continued to seek a negotiated settlement.

In retrospect it is often argued that they should have gone to war and called Hitler's bluff. Chamberlain's critics particularly stress that Russia was ready to come to the help of Czechoslovakia, but at the time offers of Russian help seemed to the British, French and even the Czechs to be unconvincing. As neither Poland nor Romania would allow Russian troops through their territory, how could they help Czechoslovakia? It is thus not surprising that Chamberlain and Daladier warmly welcomed Mussolini's last-minute proposal on 28 September for a four power conference in Munich. The next day under pressure from his generals and from Mussolini, who both dreaded a premature war, Hitler reluctantly agreed to delay the occupation of the Sudetenland until 10 October and to allow an international commission to map the boundary line. He also consented, together with Britain, France and Italy, to guarantee what remained of the independence of Czechoslovakia and signed a declaration which affirmed the desire of Britain and Germany 'never to go to war with one another again'. This was supplemented by a similar declaration signed by Ribbentrop, Hitler's Foreign Minister, in Paris in December.

It is too simple to call Munich a triumph for Hitler. He had, it is true, secured the Sudetenland, but arguably he had been cheated of his real aim, the destruction of Czechoslovakia, which apparently was now about to be protected by an international guarantee. Germany seemed to be in danger of being enmeshed in just the sort of international agreement Hitler had always hoped to avoid. However, even the most revisionist of historians would be hard put to call Munich a great victory for Chamberlain. Arguably he did buy more time for re-armament, but to the outside world Munich seemed to be a major defeat for Britain and France. The British ambassador in Tokyo reported:

> The Japanese reaction ... is that we are prepared to put up with almost any indignity rather than fight. The result is that all in all, our prestige is at a low ebb in the East....

## c) The Destruction of Czechoslovakia

The argument that Hitler merely responded to events is hard to sustain when his foreign policy from October 1938 to March 1939 is analysed. His main priority remained the destruction of

Czechoslovakia. On 21 October 1938 the German army was ordered to draw up fresh plans for military action. Simultaneously Hitler dangled the bait of territorial gains at the expense of the Czechs in front of the Hungarians, Poles and Romanians in order to enlist their support. German agents were also sent into Slovakia to fuel agitation against Prague. In practice Britain and France were already beginning to recognise Czechoslovakia as a German sphere of influence. The German representatives were allowed to dominate the international commission that was to map out the new frontiers after the secession of the Sudetenland and neither power protested when Germany refused to participate in finalising the terms of the joint guarantee of Czechoslovakia in February 1939.

On 6 March 1939 the Germans were given the opportunity finally to dismember Czechoslovakia. When the Czechs suddenly moved troops into Slovakia to crush local demands for independence, which the Nazis of course had helped stir up, Hitler persuaded the Slovaks to appeal to Berlin for assistance. On 14 March 1939 the Czech President, Hacha, was ordered to travel to Berlin where he was ruthlessly bullied into resigning the fate of his country into 'the hands of the *Führer*'. The next day German troops occupied Prague, and Slovakia was turned into a German protectorate. This action was to bring about a major diplomatic revolution in Europe.

Crowds watching German troops enter Prague, March 1939

# 5 The Anglo-French Guarantees and Attempts to Construct a Peace Front

> **KEY ISSUES** Why did Britain and France guarantee Poland, Greece and Romania?

In 1925 the British Foreign Minister had declared that the defence of the Polish Corridor was not worth the bones of one British grenadier (see page 70), yet on 30 March 1939 Britain broke decisively with its traditional foreign policy of avoiding a Continental commitment, and, together with France, guaranteed Poland against a German attack. In many ways it appeared a foolhardy and contradictory gesture as both Britain and France lacked the military power to defend Poland and had already tacitly written off eastern Europe as a German sphere of influence. A major reason for this U-turn was the speed and brutality of the German occupation of the Czech province of Bohemia on 15 March, which clearly indicated that Hitler could no longer be trusted to respect treaties and guarantees. It is also important to stress that, in the spring of 1939, the French economy and with it French self-confidence had made a strong recovery. Thus a tougher policy towards Hitler increasingly appeared to the French government to be a realistic option.

The British Government was also alarmed by panic-stricken rumours on 17 March that Hitler was about to occupy Romania and seize the oil wells there. Access to these would greatly strengthen the German war industry and enable it to survive any future British naval blockade. At first Britain aimed to contain Germany by negotiating a four-power pact with France, Russia and Poland, but given the intense suspicion with which Russia was viewed by Poland and the other eastern European states this was not a practical policy. Yet when Hitler went on to force Lithuania to hand back the former German city of Memel to the Reich on 23 March, it became even more vital to deter Hitler by any means possible. Thus Chamberlain and Daladier had little option but to announce on 31 March 1939 an immediate Anglo-French guarantee of Poland against external attack. The Polish guarantee was, however, seen as merely the first step towards constructing a comprehensive security system in eastern Europe. Chamberlain hoped to buttress it with a series of inter-locking security pacts with other eastern European and Baltic states.

When, on 7 April, Mussolini invaded Albania a similar wave of panic amongst the eastern Mediterranean states galvanised Britain and France to guarantee both Greece and Romania. In May Britain considerably strengthened its position in the eastern Mediterranean by negotiating a preliminary agreement with Turkey for mutual assistance 'in the event of an act of aggression leading to war in the Mediterranean area'. By July both Bulgaria and Yugoslavia were beginning to gravitate towards the Anglo-French 'peace bloc', but

Hitler's success in negotiating an agreement with Soviet Russia on 23 August was to deal a shattering blow to Anglo-French prestige in eastern Europe and the Balkans.

# 6 The German Break with Poland

> **KEY ISSUE** Why did Hitler decide that Poland had to be destroyed?

At first sight it is puzzling that Hitler should have gone to war with Poland in September 1939. He had, after all, signed a non-aggression pact with it in 1934 and it had helped put pressure on the Czechs during the Munich crisis. By early 1939, however, Polish subservience to Berlin was becoming increasingly vital as Hitler realised that he might have to defeat Britain and France before moving eastwards to secure 'living space' in Russia. In October 1938, and then again in January and March 1939, Hitler unsuccessfully sounded out the Poles about the return of Danzig, the construction of a road and rail link through the Corridor and about joining the Anti-Comintern Pact. In return the Poles were offered the eventual prospect of acquiring land in the Ukraine. Essentially Hitler wanted to turn Poland into a reliable satellite, but given the fate of Czechoslovakia it was precisely this status that the Poles finally rejected in March 1939. The Anglo-French guarantee of Poland, far from deterring Hitler, convinced him that Poland would have to be eliminated, even if this meant war with Britain and France. On 23 May Hitler told his generals:

> 1  Poland will always be on the side of our adversaries ... Danzig is not the objective. It is a matter of expanding our living space in the east ... We cannot expect a repetition of Czechoslovakia. There will be fighting. The task is to isolate Poland ... Basic principle: conflict with Poland,
> 5  beginning with the attack on Poland, will be successful only if the West keeps out. If that is impossible, then it is better to attack the West and finish off Poland at the same time. It will be a task of dexterous diplomacy to isolate Poland ...

# 7 The Russian Factor

> **KEY ISSUES** Why did Britain, France and Germany begin negotiations with Russia in the summer of 1939? Why did Stalin eventually decide to sign the Nazi–Soviet Pact?

Diplomatically the Nazi–Soviet Pact was a revolutionary event as significant as the British guarantee of Poland. To most contemporaries it seemed unbelievable that Hitler could negotiate an agreement with a power which he was committed to destroy. Yet in retrospect the Nazi–Soviet Pact seems almost inevitable. There were considerable advantages for Stalin in an agreement with Hitler which would keep the Soviet Union out of a war in Europe at a time when Soviet troops were fighting increasingly bitter frontier engagements against the Japanese along the Manchurian and Outer Mongolian borders. Also, the prospect of Britain, Germany and France fighting themselves to a standstill in western Europe would not only relieve the pressure on Russia, but also improve the prospects for the spread of Communism – Stalin, like the British and Americans, had, of course, no idea that France would be defeated in 6 weeks in 1940. For Hitler, once war against Poland seemed inevitable, it made good sense to ensure the support or at least neutrality of the USSR. As soon as victory was assured over Poland and the Western democracies, Soviet Russia could be dealt with.

The Anglo-French guarantee of Poland enormously strengthened Stalin's position. To build up their 'peace front' against Hitler the British and French needed a pact with Russia, but now that they were pledged to defend Poland, which was also a barrier against German expansion eastwards, Stalin could afford to play off Hitler against Chamberlain and Daladier. Protracted negotiations between Russia, Britain and France began in April 1939, but both sides deeply mistrusted each other. Stalin's demand that Russia should have the right militarily to intervene in the affairs of the small states on its western borders if they were threatened with internal subversion by the Nazis, as Austria and Czechoslovakia had been in 1938, was rejected outright by the British. They feared that the Russians would use the threat of Nazi indirect aggression as an excuse to seize the territories for themselves. Stalin, on the other hand, was equally suspicious that the Democracies were attempting to manoeuvre the Russians into a position where they would have to do most of the fighting against Germany. The British delegate, William Strang, reported:

> if we do not trust them, they equally do not trust us. They are not, fundamentally, a friendly power; but they, like us, are driven to this course by force of necessity. If we are of two minds about the wisdom of what we are doing, so are they.

The Russians thus had ample time to explore the possibility of a pact with Germany, which became genuinely interested in negotiations once the decision was taken on 23 May to prepare for war against Poland. Right through to the middle of August Moscow continued to keep both options open, but by then the slow pace of Anglo-French-Soviet military discussions seems finally to have convinced Stalin that an agreement with Hitler would be preferable. With only days to go before the start of the military campaign against Poland, Hitler was ready to accept Stalin's terms and the Soviet–Nazi Pact was signed on

23 August. Not only did the pact commit both powers to benevolent neutrality towards each other, but in a secret protocol it outlined the German and Russian spheres of interest in eastern Europe: the Baltic states and Bessarabia in Romania (see map, page 32) fell within the Russian sphere, while Poland was to be divided between the two Powers. Above all, by neutralising Soviet Russia, the pact made an attack on Poland a much less risky policy for Hitler, even if Britain and France did try to come to its rescue.

Given the deep and not entirely unjustified suspicions of Soviet Russia in Britain, France and the eastern European states, the Nazi–Soviet Pact was the most likely outcome from the tangle of negotiations that took place in the summer of 1939. It did, however, make a German attack on Poland almost inevitable.

# 8 The Outbreak of War

> **KEY ISSUE** Why did Britain go to war on behalf of Poland in 3 September 1939?

On 22 August, on the eve of the signature of the Nazi–Soviet Pact, Hitler boasted that:

WONDER HOW LONG THE HONEYMOON WILL LAST?

'Wonder How Long the Honeymoon Will Last?' *Washington Star,* 9 October 1939.

1   To be sure a new situation has arisen. I experienced those poor worms, Daladier and Chamberlain, in Munich. They will be too cowardly to attack. They won't go beyond a blockade. Against that we have autarchy [self sufficiency] and the Russian raw materials. Poland will be depopu-
5   lated and settled with Germans. My pact with the Poles was merely conceived of as a gaining of time ... After Stalin's death – he is a very sick man – we will break the Soviet Union. Then there will begin the dawn of German rule of the earth.

The omens did indeed look good for Hitler. Although he had failed to convert the Anti-Comintern Pact into a military alliance against Britain and France (see page 115), he had in May concluded the Pact of Steel with Italy by which Mussolini rashly agreed to support Germany militarily in the event of war. Neither did it appear that appeasement in Britain and France was dead. In June, Lord Halifax, the Foreign Secretary, stressed that while Britain would defend Poland against any threat to its independence, this did not necessarily mean that its existing frontiers could not be altered or the status of Danzig changed. He went on to repeat a message that was frequently to come out of London in the summer of 1939 – namely that once trust was re-established 'any of Germany's claims are open to consideration round a table'.[15] In June and July there were also sporadic talks between British and German officials on economic collaboration in Europe and Africa. In France, too, the mood seemed increasingly defeatist, and Bonnet, the French Foreign Minister, was suggesting that France should 'push Warsaw into a compromise'.[16]

Overall then Hitler had good grounds to be confident. On 23 August he ordered the army to prepare to attack Poland on the 26th, but then 2 days later these orders were cancelled because, contrary to his expectations, Britain had reacted to the news of the Nazi–Soviet Pact by ratifying its guarantee of Poland. Mussolini also announced that he could not fight without impossibly large deliveries of German armaments and equipment. Was there now a chance for a compromise? Superficially it might seem that there was. During the next few days the British and French utilised all the diplomatic channels they could to avoid war. Theoretically some sort of compromise on Poland might eventually have been possible, but in the final analysis they were not ready to sacrifice Poland's independence to achieve it. They were unwilling to repeat Munich. They wanted, as Adamthwaite has stressed, '*détente*, but negotiated from strength'. Hitler's position was diametrically opposed to this. He was insistent on first destroying Poland and only then negotiating with Britain and France. On 25 August he even offered Britain an alliance and a guarantee of its empire provided it consented to the destruction of Poland and German supremacy in eastern Europe. The response from London continued to be that only after a freely negotiated Polish–German agreement could the future of Anglo-German relations be discussed.

Belatedly it looked as if Hitler was making some concession to this position when, on 29 August, he suddenly demanded that the British should instruct the Poles to send a minister with full negotiating powers to Berlin by the following day. Fearing that Hitler would treat him as he had Schuschnigg and Hacha, the British government refused to press the Poles to send a negotiator to Berlin, and instead argued that such a deadline was impracticable since time was needed to prepare for negotiations. Was a last-minute chance to save the peace lost? Taylor argues that war began simply because Hitler launched 'on 29 August a diplomatic manoeuvre which he ought to have launched on 28 August'.[17] It is more likely, however, that Hitler was aiming to isolate Poland and to manoeuvre it into a position where its 'stubbornness' could be blamed for starting the war.

Halder, the Chief-of-Staff of the German Army, summarised Hitler's tactics:

1   Attack starts September 1st … *Führer* will let us know at once if we are
    not to strike … *Führer* very calm and clear … Plan: we demand Danzig,
    corridor through Corridor, and plebiscite on same basis as Saar.
    England will perhaps accept. Poland probably not. Wedge between
5   them!

Arguably these demands were relatively moderate, but how genuine were they? All the evidence points to Hitler's determination to destroy Poland. Even if the Poles had turned up in Berlin, the plan according to Halder was:

Basic principles: raise a barrage of demographic [relating to population] and democratic demands … 30.8. Poles in Berlin. 31.8. Blow up. 1.9. Use of force.

Even when, on 1 September 1939, Germany at last invaded Poland, frantic efforts to avert war still continued. Mussolini urged a Four-Power European Conference, and only when it was absolutely clear that Hitler would not withdraw his troops from Poland did Britain and France declare war on Germany on 3 September.

# 9 Assessment

KEY ISSUE  What were the causes of the Second World War?

Was the second world war inevitable? Was it essentially a continuation of the First World War or an entirely different conflict which competent diplomacy could have prevented? In 1918 Germany was defeated but not destroyed. It still remained potentially strong and ultimately capable of making a second attempt at dominating Europe. In that sense the Treaty of Versailles, which humiliated but did not permanently weaken

Germany, could well be seen as the 'seed bed' of the Second World War. Arguably the chain of crises which started with the *Anschluss* and ended in the German attack on Poland owed its origins to the Versailles settlement. Does it therefore follow that Versailles made war inevitable? Stresemann, Briand and Austen Chamberlain appeared for a time to be able to make the settlement work after modifying the reparation clauses. Nevertheless, it was clear that a revived Germany would still demand its drastic revision, as indeed Stresemann was already beginning to do by the late 1920s. In that sense, there was a natural continuity of aims between the Weimar Republic and the Third Reich. Yet despite Taylor's attempts to portray Hitler as a normal politician, his seizure of power in January 1933 did make a crucial difference. He gave a new and powerful impetus based on the doctrine of racial superiority to German demands for *Lebensraum* in eastern Europe. The mistake the ex-Allies made was to tolerate Hitler's expansionary policies for so long. When the time came to call a halt, it was no longer possible to do so without a major war.

To a certain extent the horrendous figure of Adolf Hitler obscures the fact that the British and French governments went to war to maintain their position as great powers rather than to wage a crusade against the evil force of Nazism. There is no doubt that Hitler's successes in eastern Europe in 1938–9 did threaten to destabilise the whole continent. After the German occupation of Bohemia the British and French governments believed that they had no choice but to oppose Hitler if they wished to maintain any influence in Europe. Of course they still kept the door open to negotiations, and pursued the increasingly vain hope of a general settlement with Germany, but essentially Britain and France were ready to risk war in 1939. Indeed the British Treasury was beginning to argue that Britain's financial position would decline after 1939, and that if war had to come it was preferable sooner rather than later. In France Daladier had steadied the economy and the aeronautical industry was rapidly expanding in early 1939.

It does seem, therefore, that Britain and France went to war in 1939 as they did in 1914 to contain Germany and safeguard their own great power status. Arguably then it was a continuation of the same struggle, even though Italy, Japan and Russia were now potential allies of the Germans. Could it be, however, as Maurice Cowling[18] argues, that Nazi Germany did not in fact threaten Britain and that it was Chamberlain who incurred German hostility by unnecessarily intervening in the Sudeten crisis in September 1938? The main thrust of Hitler's policy was certainly eastwards, but as early as November 1937, or so the Hossbach Memorandum indicates, (see page 124) he was obviously envisaging the possibility of having to fight both the Western powers. Could genuine British and French independence have survived a German victory in eastern Europe? Would Hitler have tolerated such independence without taking steps to diminish it?

# References

1 Quoted in R.J. Overy, *The Origins of the Second World War* (London, Longman, 1987), p. 22.
2 See T.W. Mason, 'Some Origins of the Second World War' in E.M. Robertson (ed.), *The Origins of the Second World War* (London, Macmillan, 1971), pp. 105–55.
3 W.M. Carr, *Arms, Autarky and Aggression* (London, Arnold, 1972) p. 65.
4 A.J.P. Taylor, *The Origins of the Second World War* (London, Arnold, 1961), p. 132
5 Carr, *Arms*, p. 128
6 'Cato', *Guilty Men*, London, 1940 (reprinted Penguin, 1998).
7 K. Robbins, *Munich*, 1938 (London, 1968); K. Middlemas, *Diplomacy of Illusion: The British Government and Germany* (London, 1972).
8 R. Shay, *British Rearmament in the Thirties: Politics and Profits* (Princeton, Princeton University Press), 1977)
9 J. Charmley, *Churchill: The End of Glory* (London, Hodder & Stoughton), 1993
10 R.A.C. Parker, *Chamberlain and Appeasement: British policy and the Coming of the Second World War* (Basingstoke, Macmillan,1993); and *Churchill and Appeasement* (London, Palgrave, 2000).
11 Quoted in S. Aster, 'Guilty Men: The Case of Neville Chamberlain' in R. Boyce and E.M. Robertson (eds), *Paths to War* (Basingstoke, Macmillan, 1989), p. 246.
12 Taylor, *Origins*, p. 152.
13 A. Bullock, 'Hitler and the Origins of the Second World War' in E.M. Robertson (ed.), *Origins*, p. 208
14 Taylor, *Origins*, p. 179.
15 A.P. Adamthwaite, *The Making of the Second World War* (London, Allen and Unwin, 1977), p. 91.
16 Quoted in Taylor, *Origins*, p. 264.
17 Ibid., p278.
18 M. Cowling, *The Impact of Hitler*, Cambridge, CUP, 1975.

## Summary Diagram
The Countdown to War

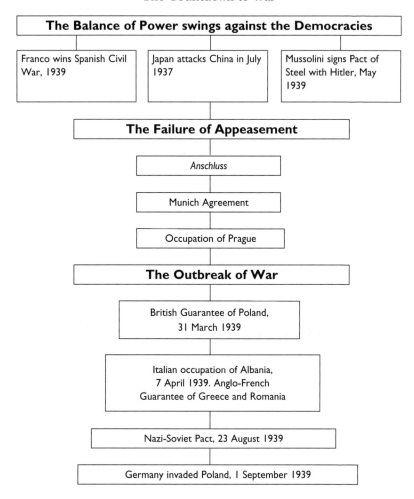

---

**Working on Chapter 6**

This chapter covers the crucial two years before the outbreak of the
Second World War. In making notes you need, first of all, to be clear
about the global pressures on Britain and France. Thus while you
read about how Britain and France tried to contain Nazi Germany,
you need to bear in mind the possible impact of the Sino-Japanese
war on their Far Eastern empires. Similarly, nearer home, Italy's
increasingly closer relations with Berlin also threatened the Anglo-
French position in the Mediterranean. An understanding of these

pressures will help you understand why Britain and France tried initially to pursue a policy of appeasement. It is important that you make your mind up about the pros and cons of appeasement, but make sure that you first of all understand what the word means!

A key question to consider is whether Hitler could in fact be appeased without Britain and France completely surrendering their remaining influence in Europe. What were Hitler's aims? Was he just an opportunist, as Taylor argues, or did he have a programme, as the Hossbach Memorandum seems to indicate? You will need to note the action-packed period from the *Anschluss* to the outbreak of war very carefully. Ask yourself why Britain and France accepted the *Anschluss* and the handing over of the Sudetenland, yet after the destruction of rump Czechoslovakia in March 1939 pursued a much tougher line towards Nazi Germany, which involved the guarantee of Poland, Greece and Romania. Had Hitler finally exhausted the patience of the two western powers after the destruction of Czechoslovakia? Were Britain and France at last ready to fight to preserve what little was left of the Versailles settlement? Finally you need to look carefully at the period April–September 1939? Before you write up your notes, ask yourself, carefully, why Stalin signed the Nazi–Soviet Pact and not an alliance with Britain and France. Did this make the war over Poland unavoidable?

## Answering Structured and essay questions on Chapter 6

1 **a)** Outline briefly what Hitler's programme for expansion was, as recorded in the Hossbach Memorandum.
   **b)** How successfully was Hitler able to implement this programme by September 1939?
2 **a)** Explain what the policy of appeasement was in the 1930s.
   **b)** Why did it fail?
3 **a)** Explain why Britain and France guaranteed Poland in March 1939.
   **b)** Why did this guarantee not stop Hitler attacking Poland in September 1939?

Part a) of these questions again primarily tests your factual knowledge and comprehension of events. The three part b) questions are testing your ability to interpret the facts and come to a judgement based on them. Thus 1b) requires you to assess *how far* Hitler had implemented his programme by September 1939. In doing this you need to consider whether Hitler really had a programme or whether he was just lucky! 2b) entails an analysis of the failures of appeasement in the period 1937–9, while 3b) involves an analysis of why war broke out in September 1939.

Since questions on the causes of the Second World War are frequently set, it is vital that you should be able to analyse the origins of the war from every angle. You will therefore need to re-read your notes on Chapters 1–5. Questions can be very detailed and focus on events in 1939 or they can be more general and require you to show an understanding of the whole interwar era.

Study the following questions which are a mixture of both types of question:

1 Why did the Second World War break out over Poland rather than over Czechoslovakia?
2 'The second round of the conflict that ended in November 1918 began in September 1939'. How well does this sum up the causes of the Second World War?
3 Why could German expansion eastwards not be prevented?
4 Why did appeasement work in the 1920s but fail in the 1930s?
5 To what extent can it be argued that Hitler was planning a European War in 1939?
6 'The Nazi–Soviet Pact, far from being a surprise, was inevitable'. Discuss.
7 To what extent can the Anglo-French failure to halt Nazi aggression in the period March 1938–March 1939 be accounted for by the existence of the Rome–Berlin Axis and the Anti-Comintern Pact?

You can see from these questions that examiners can approach questions on the causes of the Second World War in a number of different ways. Arguably the most straightforward, but not necessarily the easiest, approach is a direct question on why war broke out as in Question 1. Before you answer this, draw up a list of all the reasons why you think war broke out in September 1939 rather than in September 1938 or March 1939. Was Poland the real cause of the war or the 'last straw' for the western powers? Question 2 invites you to consider the long-term causes. You should consider this explanation in light of the list of causes you have drawn up. You may come to the conclusion that, far from being round two, it was in fact 'Hitler's war', or, on the other hand, you may come to the conclusion that it was a mixture of both. The examiner often sets questions on the relationship between Hitler's aims and Anglo-French appeasement. In Questions 3 and 4 how would you strike the balance between the weaknesses inherent in appeasement and Hitler's responsibility for the war? To answer Question 6, you need to bear in mind Russia's relations with Germany, Britain and France from the Revolution onwards, if you are to understand Stalin's thinking. You have, of course also to account for the paradox of Hitler, the great anti-Bolshevik, apparently entering into partnership with Soviet Russia. In Question 7 the examiner raises the difficult question of the impact of both the Rome–Berlin Axis and the Anti-Comintern Pact on Anglo-French policy. Here you need to explore whether these pacts really represented a realignment of the powers. Significantly, neither Italy nor Japan declared war in September 1939, but on the other hand they were a potential combination against Britain and France and so inevitably acted as both a distraction and a threat. Can you find the evidence in Chapter 6 to support this argument?

## Source-based questions on Chapter 6

**1** **The Outbreak of the Sino-Japanese War**
Carefully read the extracts from the French diplomat's report (Source A) on page 122 and Roosevelt's 'quarantine speech' (Source B) on page 122. Answer the following questions:
**a)** Study Source A
What is meant by 'the present tensions ... in Europe' (line 1)? (*3 marks*)
**b)** Study Source B
What does Roosevelt mean when he calls war a 'contagion' (line 1)? (*2 marks*)
**c)** Study Sources A and B and use your own knowledge
Explain Why Britain and France were powerless to stop Japanese expansion in the Far East. (*10 marks*)

**2** **The Hossbach Memorandum, November 1937**
Carefully read the extract on page 124 (Source A). Answer the following questions:
**a)** What was Germany's 'question of space' (lines 2–3)? (2 marks)
**b)** Why was it so important to solve this problem by 1943–5 (line 16)? (*3 marks*)
**c)** As 'Contingencies 2 and 3' (lines 21–34) did not happen, does this mean that the Hossbach Memorandum has little value as a guide to Hitler's foreign policy? Explain why you agree or disagree with this proposition. (*10 marks*)

**3** **Appeasement and the Munich Crisis, 1938**
Carefully read the extracts from Chamberlain's two statements on pages 127 and 130 (Sources A and B) and the British Ambassador's report from Tokyo on page 132 (Source C) and study the illustrations on page 131 and 133 (Sources D and E). Answer the following questions:
**a)** Study Source A and use your own knowledge
Explain what Chamberlain's policy towards Germany was in November 1937. (*5 marks*)
**b)** Study Sources A, B and D and use your own knowledge
Explain why Chamberlain was determined to prevent war over the Sudetenland. (*10 marks*)
**c)** Study all the Sources and use your own knowledge.
Examine the view that Munich was in fact a major defeat for Britain and France. (*15 marks*)

**4** **The Outbreak of War, 1939**
Carefully read Hitler's address on 23 May to his generals on page 135 (Source A), his statement of 22 August on page 138 (Source B), Halder's summary of his tactics on page 139 (Source C), the extract from Strang's report (Source D) on page 136 and study the cartoon on page 137 (Source E).
**a)** Study Source A and use your own knowledge
Explain what Hitler means by 'we cannot expect a repetition of Czechoslovakia' (lines 2–3)? (*5 marks*).

**b)** Study Source E and use your own knowledge
Explain briefly the significance of the way in which Hitler and Stalin are represented as a bridal pair. (*5 marks*)

**c)** Study Sources A and B and use your own knowledge
To what extent does Source B indicate that Hitler had achieved his aims concerning Poland by 22 August? (*10 marks*)

**d)** Study all the Sources and use your own knowledge.
Examine the view that Hitler did not believe that Britain and France would go to war over Poland. (*10 marks*)

# 7 Conclusion: The Interwar Years in Retrospect

## POINTS TO CONSIDER

This chapter is a general survey of the interwar period concentrating on the issues which anybody studying the period needs to think about. Your aim should be to consolidate your overall knowledge and understanding of the whole period with particular focus on key problems and trends.

## 1 The Peace Treaties

**KEY ISSUE** How open to criticism are the peace treaties?

After the Second World War the peace treaties of 1919–20 were blamed for the rise of Hitler and the Second World War. In its millennium issue a prestigious London weekly, *The Economist*, described the Treaty of Versailles as the 'final crime of the twentieth century... whose harsh terms would ensure a second world war'.[1] Yet in so many ways Versailles was a compromise peace: the German Reich, which had only been created in 1871, was left intact, and with the disintegration of the Austro-Hungarian and Russian empires in eastern Europe, its position was in fact in the medium to long term strengthened. As the German historian Karl Erdmann observed, it was either too lenient or too severe:

> Too severe, since Germany could do no other, from the first moment onwards, than try to shake it off; too lenient, because Germany was not so weakened as to be deprived of the hope and possibility of either extricating herself from the treaty or tearing it up.

The other peace treaties are arguably even harder to defend. Sèvres had to be revised under threat of war with a revived nationalist Turkey led by Kemal. St Germain, Neuilly and Trianon attempted to create a series of states in the Balkans and South Eastern Europe, along the lines suggested in the 14 Points. This involved, however, attempting to create nation states where there was no ethnic unity. By 1942 Nazi Germany had annexed Austria, and destroyed both Czechoslovakia and Yugoslavia. After the defeat of Germany in 1945 the latter two states were restored, and ethnic conflicts were kept under control by Communist regimes, but with the end of the Cold war in 1989 both Czechoslovakia and Yugoslavia disintegrated in the early 1990s.

## 2 The New Global Balance of Power after the Peace Treaties

> **KEY ISSUE** How stable was the new balance of power created by the peace treaties?

In 1919 America emerged from the First World War as the dominant world financial power. At this stage, however, the USA still lacked the will to play the role of a great power. The refusal of the Republican-dominated Senate to ratify the Treaty of Versailles ensured that the USA remained on the sidelines of international politics until 1924.

This placed France in a paradoxical position. As a consequence of Germany's defeat and America's return to isolation, it had become by default the world's greatest military power, but it was not a role that it could sustain.

In 1919 Russia, like Germany, had been a defeated power. The peace treaties had, in effect, been imposed on Russia as they were on Germany, Austria, Hungary, Bulgaria and Turkey. It had not been consulted about the borders of Turkey or of Poland. After the Bolshevik victory in the civil war, the Soviet Union's greatest priority was to defend the revolution and modernise the economy.

Like France in 1919, Britain still outwardly appeared to be a great power, but it was a status that it could not sustain, as its economy had been fatally weakened in the war.

Japan made considerable gains at Versailles where it was able to increase its influence in China and in the Pacific at Germany's expense, and it was also given a permanent seat on the Council of the League of Nations. However, as the Treaty of Washington showed, it was still regarded as a junior partner to the USA and Britain in the Far East.

Apart from benefiting from the destruction of the Austro-Hungarian Empire, which dominated its northern frontiers, Italy gained little from the peace treaties. It could not achieve its territorial ambitions in Africa and the Balkans until it could play off the western powers against Germany, a situation which was only possible after Hitler's rise to power.

## 3 Anglo-French Rivalry and the Attempts to Enforce the Treaty

> **KEY ISSUE** What were the reasons for the rivalry between Britain and France, 1919–24?

The rejection of the Treaty and Covenant of the League by the American Senate had grave consequences for the long-term peace of

Europe. France was deprived of the vital Anglo-American treaty of guarantee, which would have given it security, and had therefore ruthlessly to exploit its temporary dominance over Germany. Over the course of the next 4 years it used every opportunity to weaken Germany and, where possible, to re-interpret the clauses of the Treaty so that they would do the maximum harm to Germany, while Britain adopted a contrary view and tried to preserve an economically viable Germany, which would be able both to pay reparations and act as a motor for the recovery of the European economy.

The crucial trial of strength not only between Germany and France but also between the British and French governments came with the occupation of the Ruhr in 1923–4 by French and Belgian troops. Britain distanced itself through a policy of 'benevolent passivity', while Germany pursued a policy of passive resistance. By September the cost of this resistance, which had triggered hyper-inflation, forced Germany to come to terms with France, but by now France was determined to create a Rhineland independent of Germany. Whether it succeeded or not depended on the strength of the franc, the attitude of the Rhinelanders and the policy pursued by London and Washington, which emerged from isolation to play an important role in the reconstruction of Germany's finances through the Dawes plan. By early 1924 it was becoming increasingly clear that France could not win support for an independent Rhineland, and with a rapidly collapsing franc had little option but to accept the Dawes Plan.

# 4 The Fragile Stabilisation, 1924–9

> **KEY ISSUE** Why was the period of stabilisation, 1924–9, so short lived?

At the end of the First World War European prosperity could not be rebuilt until America partially re-emerged from isolation to assist in restoring European finances after the French occupation of the Ruhr had triggered hyper-inflation in Germany and also seriously weakened the franc. The brief stabilisation of the European economy that occurred between 1924 and 1929 had some similarities with the stabilisation of the western European economy after 1948. In 1924 a fragile economic and diplomatic equilibrium was created as a consequence of the Dawes Plan and the Locarno Agreements. As in 1948, American money did flow into Germany and help revive the economy. Confidence was further strengthened by a growing trust between France and Germany symbolised by the Briand–Stresemann relationship and the increasing talk about a European union, which to some extent anticipated the debates of the 1950s. Are historians, then, correct to see the 1920s as a 'darkening twilight of the liberal era'? One American scholar, Charles S. Maier,[2] points out that this period was in fact a time of new ideas for economic and political cooperation, which could have provided an escape from great power conflict. Indeed he argues that if it was a 'twilight decade, the 1920s was one of morning as well as dusk'. The crucial difference, however, between the two postwar periods is that in the 1920s the financing of the European economy was left to private investors, mainly American, while in the late-1940s, through Marshall Aid, investment was guaranteed by the American state itself and was therefore more secure.

## 5 Did the Great Depression make the Second World War Inevitable?

> **KEY ISSUE** Why was the impact of the Depression on international politics so disastrous?

Even Marshall Aid might have faltered in the face of a recession on the scale of the Great Depression of 1929–30. Most historians agree that the Depression was a pre-condition for the rise of Hitler and the success of Japanese militarism in the Far East and thus a major cause of the Second World War. On the other hand, if you believe that there was a continuity in German foreign policy, and that the Second World War was merely a renewal of Germany's attempt to dominate Europe in the First World war, the significance of the Depression needs to be downgraded perhaps.

The Depression was, however, instrumental in pushing America back into isolation just when Europe most needed it. German and Japanese expansion in the 1930s were facilitated by American inactivity in the Far East and the failure of the Anglo-French policy of appeasement in Europe. Only in March 1939, when Hitler occupied Bohemia and Britain guaranteed Poland, did it become quite clear that Britain could not tolerate unlimited German expansion in eastern Europe. The last chance of deterring Hitler was destroyed when Stalin opted for the Nazi–Soviet Pact, rather than a military alliance with Britain and France, in order to regain some of Russia's former Polish territory. Were the events that led to war in 1938–9 inevitable? What role did miscalculation or just bad luck play in their unfolding? If you are convinced that Hitler was determined on war, then you will clearly be very sceptical of Taylor's argument that there was nothing inevitable about the outbreak of the European war in September 1939[3]. On the other hand, would a crucial difference have been made, if Britain and France could have kept Italy on their side or negotiated a successful alliance with Soviet Russia? Is there any truth in the argument that the British feared Stalin more than they did Hitler? An even more important question is the role of appeasement.

Was it, as many of the revisionist historians argue, the only rational policy open to Britain and France, given the hostility of Italy and Japan, or could Chamberlain have pursued a different policy, as R.A.C. Parker[4] has indicated, of building up an alliance against Nazi Germany in the name of the League of Nations?

## References

1  *The Economist*, 31 December 1999, quoted in M. Macmillan, *Peacemakers* (London, Murray, 2001), p. 499.
2  C. Maier, *Recasting Bourgeois Europe* (Princeton, Princeton University Press, 1988 edition), p. 594.
3  A.J.P. Taylor, *The Origins of the Second World War* (London, Hamish Hamilton, 1961).
4  R.A.C. Parker. *Chamberlain and Appeasement* (Basingstoke, Macmillan, 1993).

### Summary Diagram

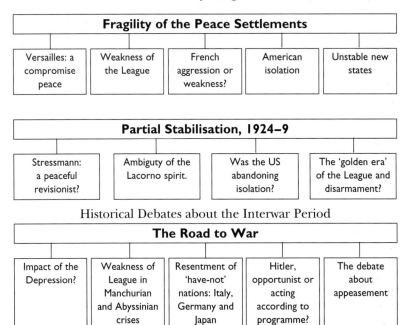

| Fragility of the Peace Settlements | | | | |
|---|---|---|---|---|
| Versailles: a compromise peace | Weakness of the League | French aggression or weakness? | American isolation | Unstable new states |

| Partial Stabilisation, 1924–9 | | | |
|---|---|---|---|
| Stressmann: a peaceful revisionist? | Ambiguty of the Lacorno spirit. | Was the US abandoning isolation? | The 'golden era' of the League and disarmament? |

Historical Debates about the Interwar Period

| The Road to War | | | | |
|---|---|---|---|---|
| Impact of the Depression? | Weakness of League in Manchurian and Abyssinian crises | Resentment of 'have-not' nations: Italy, Germany and Japan | Hitler, opportunist or acting according to programme? | The debate about appeasement |

### Working on Chapter 7

There is no need to make any detailed notes on this chapter, but it is important to consider what key themes keep repeating themselves in this book and why they do so. You need to make up your mind about two main groups of questions:

**1** The role of Germany, 1919–39. Is this the central issue of the period?
**2** Are therefore all the other issues, such as Italian and Japanese imperialism, the emergence of America as a great power which refused to engage fully in international affairs, British and French decline, the impact of the Depression, the role of Soviet Russia and the attempts to create a system of collective security, essentially only of secondary importance and to be analysed only in relation to Germany?

To answer these questions you must decide on your criteria. How do you define a 'central issue'? Is it one that ultimately dominates all other issues, so that they seem both to contemporaries and historians to be of subordinate importance to the central problem?

Once you have decided on your criteria, you will need to look back at your notes on the preceding chapters and follow the developments of the various issues listed above. Whatever you decide about the role Germany played in this period, you will need to analyse the attempts by the European powers and America to contain it through treaties, appeasement and financial concessions during the period 1919–39. Whilst doing this, you may then well come to the conclusion that the German problem only dominated because, for example, the Russian Revolution temporarily upset the European balance of power or that it was only a consequence of the Depression. Whatever your conclusions, you will need to have an overall grasp of the period covered by this book and opinions of your own on the historical debates which many aspects of these troubled years have given rise to. You should then be able to face the examiner with confidence!

When you have thought through these problems, consider the following examples of essays questions, which cover the whole period:

**1** How consistent was British policy towards Germany, 1919–39?
**2** Was the Second World War in any sense inevitable?
**3** 'In the interwar period Britain and France were great powers by default'. Discuss this statement in reference to American isolationism.

All three question involve drawing on the interwar period as a whole. To answer Question 1 you will need to analyse Britain's attitude towards Germany at the Peace Conference and in the immediate post-war period. Britain did not want Germany destroyed, as it was a potentially valuable trading partner as well as a barrier against Bolshevism. Thus Britain was ready to make concessions in the early 1920s to 'appease' Germany. The logic of this policy continued on until 1938. Only in the spring of 1939, when the scale of Hitler's ambitions became clear, did Britain take the radical step of guaranteeing Poland and considering war against Germany as the means for defending its position in Europe.

Question 2 is the key issue in this book. Could the German problem have been solved peacefully in 1919, thus saving Europe from the terrible suffering of the years 1939–45? If America had not suffered from 'stage fright' in 1919 and abdicated from the role of a great power, history might have run a different course. For a start, the Anglo-American guarantee of France would have been in place, and France would not have been driven to ensure its own security by exploiting the Treaty of Versailles. America would also have played a key role in the League of Nations. However, should the USA in default be cast as the villain of the interwar period? The USA did, after all, contribute to the financial recovery of Europe after 1924, and considerable progress was made towards a peaceful revision of the Treaty of Versailles. It is certainly possible to argue that the Depression did more than anything else to make the Second World War possible, as it weakened the democracies and brought Hitler to power. Yet even then could Britain, as R.A.C. Parker has argued, have built up a European alliance which might have contained Hitler? Perhaps decisive action, possibly in 1936 when the Rhineland was remilitarised, might have deterred Hitler; but here we are in the realms of 'virtual' history!

Question 3 is difficult. Initially you need to show how America, after playing a key role in the peace negotiations in Paris, was prevented from joining the League or helping to implement the treaty by the Senate. This inevitably left Britain and France supreme in Europe. Is this what 'great powers by default' means? This implies that, had America been present in the League and represented on the inter-Allied commissions carrying out the peace treaties, both countries would have played a more subordinate role. Certainly both Britain and France had to bow to American wishes in the Pacific when they signed the Washington Treaty in 1922. Ultimately America was also able to persuade both France and Germany to accept the Dawes Plan, and to take a leading role in negotiating the Young Plan. However, the Depression caused the second and more total withdrawal of the USA into isolation, and left Britain and France alone to face Germany, Italy and Japan. They had to fill the role of great powers, but lacked the strength to do so.

# Glossary

| | |
|---|---|
| *Anschluss* | The union of Austria with Germany. |
| **Appeasement** | The conciliation of a potential enemy by making concessions. The term is particularly applied to Neville Chamberlain's policy towards Nazi Germany. |
| **Armistice** | An agreement to end hostilities, so that peace negotiations can begin. |
| **Austria-Hungary** | The Austrian Empire, as it was called after 1867. |
| **Axis Powers** | Nazi Germany's allies. |
| **Bolsheviks** | The Russian Communist party, which seized power in Russia in October 1917. |
| **Buffer state** | A small state lying between two much larger and potentially hostile powers. By keeping them apart, it helps keep the peace. |
| **Comintern** | the Communist international movement set up in 1919. |
| **Conference of Ambassadors** | This was set up in January 1920 in Paris to ensure that the peace treaties were carried out. It consisted of the British, Italian and Japanese ambassadors and was chaired by a French official. |
| **Customs Union** | An economic bloc, the members of which trade freely with each other. |
| *Détente* | A condition of lessened tension or growing relaxation between two states. |
| **Depression** | The global economic slump that hit Germany and Japan particularly badly, 1930–3. |
| **Dominions** | The British Dominions of Australia, Canada, New Zealand and South Africa were self-governing, but part of the British Empire and Commonwealth, of which to this day they are still members. |
| *Freikorps* | The volunteer groups formed in Germany to defend the government against Bolshevism and against the Poles in the east. |
| *Führer* | Leader, the term used by Hitler to denote his absolute leadership of Germany and the Nazi Party. |
| **Habsburg** | The ruling dynasty of the Austrian Empire until 1918. |
| **Isolationism** | A policy which avoids alliances and joining such organisations as the League of Nations. |
| **Kaiser** | The German Emperor. |
| **Left-wing** | Political parties on the Left, that is Liberals, Socialists and (far Left) Communists. |

| | |
|---|---|
| **Locarno spirit** | The optimistic mood of reconciliation and compromise that swept through Europe after the signing of the Locarno Agreements. |
| **Mandate** | Ex-German or Turkish territories entrusted by the League of Nations to one of the Allied powers to govern in accordance to the interests of the native population. |
| **Milliard** | One thousand million. |
| **Moratorium** | A temporary suspension in debt repayments. |
| **Multilateral** | A term used to describe an agreement or policy in which more than three states are involved. |
| **Nation-state** | A state consisting of an ethnically and culturally united population, such as Italy and France. |
| **Nationalism** | A patriotic belief by a people in the virtues and power of their nation. Extreme nationalism, as in Nazi Germany, involves the desire to strengthen the state at the cost of its neighbours. |
| **Nazi** | The National Socialist German Workers' Party, which under Hitler took power in Germany in 1933. |
| **Non-aggression Pact** | An agreement signed between two or more states not to resort to force. |
| **Plebiscite** | A referendum or vote on a single issue |
| **Powers, the Great** | A term used to describe the most powerful nations, but 'power' can be used to describe any state. |
| *Rapprochement* | The development of good relations between states. |
| **Ratification** | The approval of a treaty by parliament. Without this process the treaty does not come into force. |
| **Reparations** | Compensation paid by a defeated power to make good the damage it committed in a war. |
| **Revisionist** | Somebody who revises an accepted idea or policy. Hence a revisionist historian is one who challenges the accepted, orthodox historical arguments. |
| **Right** | Term used to denote parties stretching from Conservative to Nazi or Fascist (extreme Right).. |
| **Sanctions** | Action taken by a state or the League of Nations to compel a power to accept an international agreement or to stop an unpopular policy. |
| **Sino-** | Chinese. Used in combination with another word, as in Sino-Japanese war, for example. |
| *Status Quo* | A Latin term to denote the situation as it exists at the moment. |
| **USSR** | Union of Soviet Socialist Republics. This was the Bolshevik name for Russia. |
| **White Russians** | The anti-Bolshevik and pro-Tsarist forces in the Russian civil war. |

# Further Reading

There are thousands of books on this period in many different languages. If you are looking for a good introductory survey, you will find the following studies very helpful:

M. **Kitchen**, *Europe between the Wars*, Longman, 1988.
M. **Lamb and N. Tarling**, *From Versailles To Pearl Harbor*, Palgrave, 2001.
R. **Overy**, The Inter-War Crisis, 1919–39, Longman, 1994.
R. **Parker**, *Europe, 1919–45*, Weidenfeld and Nicolson, 1969.
E. **Wiskemann**, *Europe of the Dictators, 1919–1945*, Fontana, 1966.

## The Peace Treaties

R. **Henig**, *Versailles and After, 1919–1933*, Routledge, 2nd edition 1995, is by far the best introductory guide to the Treaties and the period up to 1933.
G. **Schulz**, *Revolutions and Peace Treaties, 1917–20*, Methuen, 1972, is a helpful survey of all the treaties. Above all, it does not neglect the Russian and German dimensions.
A.J. **Mayer**, *Politics and Diplomacy in Peacemaking: Containment and Counter-Revolution at Versailles*, Weidenfeld and Nicolson, 1968, is a very detailed but readable book on the negotiation of the peace treaty. It is particularly good on developments in Russia in 1918–20.
M. **Macmillan**, *Peacemakers*, Murray, 2001 is another long but very readable and informative study on the Peace Conference.

## The Enforcement of the Treaty, the Locarno Era and the League of Nations

M. **Gilbert**, *Roots of Appeasement*, Weidenfeld and Nicolson, 1966, has some interesting chapters on appeasement in the 1920s.
J. **Jacobson**, *Locarno Diplomacy. Germany and the West, 1925–29*, Princeton University Press, 1972, is a more specialised study of the Locarno era.
W.M. **Jordan**, *Great Britain, France and the German Problem, 1918–39*, Cass, 2nd edition 1971, is certainly dated, but still admirably clear on the complicated period of 1920–5.
W.A. **McDougall**, *France's Rhineland Diplomacy, 1914–24*, Princeton UP, 1978, is a very detailed but clear guide to French policy in the Rhine in the lead-up to the Ruhr crisis.
F.S. **Northedge**, *The League of Nations, Its Life and Times*, Leicester University Press, 1986, is by far the best book on the League of Nations and is an indispensable guide to students.

**Cambridge Modern History**, Vol XII, Chapter IX, Cambridge University Press, 2nd edition, 1968, contains a short history of the League. It is not easy reading, but it is informative.

# The 1930s and the causes of the Second World War

There are an enormous number of books on the diplomacy of the 1930s and the causes of the Second World War.

**A.J.P. Taylor**, *The Origins of the Second World War*, Hamish Hamilton, 1961, is a classic which still has the power to surprise the reader. In many ways it continues to determine the framework for the debate about the outbreak of the war.

**P.M.H. Bell**, *The Second World War in Europe*, Longman,1986, is a particularly useful book, which puts the war into its political and economic context.

**R. Overy**, *The Origins of the Second World War*, Pearson, 1998, is short, well written and very much to the point.
Overy is also good on the economic dimension.

**E.M. Robertson** (ed.), *The Origins of the Second World War*, Macmillan, 1971, takes Taylor's ideas as a focus point for a debate. There are particularly useful essays by Bullock and Mason in this volume.

**R. Boyce and E.M. Robertson** (eds), *Paths to War: New essays on the Origins of the Second World War*, Macmillan, 1989, is less obsessed by Taylor's arguments and contains a series of excellent essays. It is particularly important to read R. Boyce's essay, 'Some Economic Origins of the Second World War' (Chapter 2).

**G. Martel** (ed.), *The Origins of The Second World War Reconsidered*, Routledge, 1986, contains a further set of important essays on different aspects of the interwar years.

**I. Lukes and E. Goldstein** (eds), *The Munich Crisis, 1938*, London, Cass, 1999, is a collection of essays examining different aspects of the Munich Crisis.

**D. Dutton**, *Neville Chamberlain, Arnold, 2001*, studies the reputation of Chamberlain, and much of the book is given over to the problem of appeasement and the historical controversies about it.

# Foreign Policy, of the Individual States, 1933–9

## Germany

**J. Hiden**, *Germany and Europe, 1919–39*, Longman, 2nd edition, 1993, covers the whole period and also has a good analysis of Anglo-French-German relations.

**W. Carr**, *Arms, Autarky and Aggression: A Study in German Foreign Policy, 1933–39*, Arnold, 1979, is a concise but scholarly account. It has a useful chapter on the impact of Nazi ideology on foreign policy.

**D.G. Williamson**, *The Third Reich*, Harlow, Longman, 3rd edition, 2002 and **G. Layton**, *Germany: The Third Reich*, Access Series Hodder, 2nd edition, 2000, both have relevant chapters on Nazi foreign policy.

**G.L. Weinberg**, *The Foreign Policy of Hitler's Germany*, 2 vols, University of Chicago Press, 1970 and 1980, is by far the most authoritative and detailed study.

## Britain

**A. Farmer**, *Britain: Foreign and Imperial relations, 1919–39*, Access Series, 2nd edition, 2000.

**J. Charmley**, *Chamberlain and the Lost Peace*, Macmillan, 1989, is a sympathetic defence of Chamberlain.

**R.A.C. Parker**, *Chamberlain and Appeasement: British Policy and the Coming of the Second War*, Macmillan, 1993, provides the opposite view.

**F. McDonough**, *Neville Chamberlain, Appeasement and the British Road to War*, Manchester University Press, 1998 is a more concise study of the years 1937–9.

## Italy

A detailed study of Italian foreign policy over this period is **C.J. Lowe and F. Mazari**, *Italian Foreign Policy, 1870–1940*, Routledge, 1975.

## France

**J. Neré**, The Foreign Policy of France from 1914 to 1945, Routledge, 1975, provides a clear overall account.

**A. Adamthwaite**, *France and the Coming of the Second World War, 1936–9*, Cass, 1977, is indispensable if you need to look more carefully at French policy on the eve of the Second World War.

## Spain

H. Thomas, *The Spanish Civil War*, Penguin, 1965, is the classic but very detailed account of the struggle.

H. Browne, *Spain's Civil War*, Longman, 1983 is a much shorter account.

## USSR

G.F. Kennan, *Soviet Foreign Policy, 1917–1941*, Greenwood Press, 1978, is still the best short analysis of Soviet Foreign policy.

**G. Roberts**, *The Soviet Union and the Origins of The Second World War, 1933–41*, Macmillan, 1995, is much more detailed and takes the line that the USSR wanted to build up a collective defence against Hitler.

## USA

**A. Decondes**, *A History of American Foreign Policy, vol ii*, Charles Scribner, 3rd edition, 1978, provides the best overall survey of American foreign policy.

**C. MacDonald**, *The United States, Britain and Appeasement, 1936–39*, Macmillan, 1981, is an interesting study of the USA's attitude towards appeasement.

## Japan

**W.G. Beasley**, *The Rise of Modern Japan*, London, Weidenfeld and Nicolson, 1990 is a general introduction to modern Japanese history and has some chapters on foreign policy.

**J. B. Crowley**, *Japan's Quest for Autonomy: National Security and Foreign Policy, 1930–38*, Princeton, Princeton UP, 1966 is still the best overall study of Japanese foreign policy in the 1930s.

# Sources

**A.P. Adamthwaite**, *The Making of the Second World War*, Allen and Unwin, 1979.

There are also useful collections of documents in the books mentioned above by **Kennan, Lowe** and **Mazari, Neré, Overy** and **Williamson**.

# Index